Hi,

Thank you for the purchase of this workbook. Doing simple drawings with pen and ink is a very relaxing and enjoyable hobby, and with this workbook, you will soon discover how easy it is as well.

Pen and ink drawing books usually start with detailed explanation of pen choices followed by different pen strokes and so on and by the time beginners get to actual drawing part, they are sufficiently discouraged. This workbook takes a different approach.

Main aim of this workbook is to help you get started quickly with fully illustrated explanations and hands on exercises. Text is kept to minimum. Key pen stroke and technique to render different elements of nature is clearly demonstrated and this is followed by hands on exercises for you to attempt.

Do try different activities in the workbook. You can supplement it by additional practice on your own drawing book. If the initial attempt is not to your liking, then try again. Don't get discouraged in the beginning and take break between attempts if you need to.

Once you start, you will discover the joy of putting pen on paper and creating simple pleasing landscapes from your imagination. Do feel free to reach out to me to share any questions, comments on the workbook or even your attempts along your pen and ink drawing adventure.

Happy Drawing,

Rahul Jain

www.pendrawings.me

Note on Pen and Paper:

So, what is a good pen for drawing?

Quite frankly, in the beginning, any good 'gel' pen will do, kind you will find in any local stationary shop. Choose one with fine tip (0.5mm wide or less) if you can find one. Gel pens for writing are often medium tip (0.7 mm) and their lines are often too thick to get good texture. As you progress in your journey and you desire better quality pens for drawing, you can check out my website and videos for more information.

www.pendrawings.me/penpaperchoices

Another great option is 'fine liners', which you can easily find with fine tip. One very popular brand is 'Pigma Micron', but to reiterate, any good fine point gel pen or marker/fine liner will do in the beginning.

I would suggest not using pencil. Most pencils don't give sufficiently dark lines that you need to create texture with lines alone. Permanence of pen lines also promote good observation and avoid 'draw-erase-draw' cycle that frustrates many beginners. Use of ordinary ball pen is also discouraged as their ink is not dark enough to enable proper texturing.

Most importantly, make sure that you don't get discouraged from trying activities in this workbook because you don't have a 'good quality' pen.

As for paper, in addition to this workbook, any normal paper like the one you use for normal printing will do. Avoid textured paper as this will interfere with flow of nib. Choose a smooth paper instead. There is again an incredible variety of paper available for drawing and you can find discussion on relative merits of these for pen and ink drawing at the above link.

Note on Proper Use of Pen for Drawing:

A key aspect of drawing with pen is to let your pen float on the paper with the nib/tip touching and releasing ink.

Never dig into the paper by pressing nib/tip in the paper.

Hold your pen lightly and release the tension in your hand. This will help you get the freedom of pen movement and lightness that contributes to good drawing practice.

A good quality gel pen and marker will provide a nice line with gentle touch on paper. If you find that you need to dig to get the ink out, then change the pen. 'Forcing' ink out of pen is never recommended. It will ruin drawing paper and create hard lines and ruin the drawing experience for you.

In the following pages, different pen strokes are illustrated that can be used to convey different textures. When attempting them, keep your hand supple and most importantly, keep it moving. The stroke shouldn't be done in a slow and deliberate manner, as this makes it rigid and un appealing. At the same time, don't rush through it. Find your speed and rhythm at which the pen line has a natural appeal. This takes time and practice and you will soon find yours.

For more information visit www.pendrawings.me/getstarted

Please note that all drawings and content in this workbook is my copy right and solely provided for your own personal use. It can't be used, resold or redistributed in any manner without my prior consent for any purpose other than personal use. As a pen and ink artist, my aim is to promote pen and ink drawing as a creative and relaxing hobby for all but please make sure that you obtain my consent before using the material in this workbook in any manner other than personal use.

For other workbooks in this series, please visit www.pendrawings.me/workbooks

Dedicated to all who seek to discover and express their creative side

Version 2, February 2022

Do make use of all the space in this workbook and practice doing all the activities. As with mostly everything else, practice is the key to improving. If you don't like your initial attempt, then don't get discouraged and try again. Enjoy the process of discovering your creative side

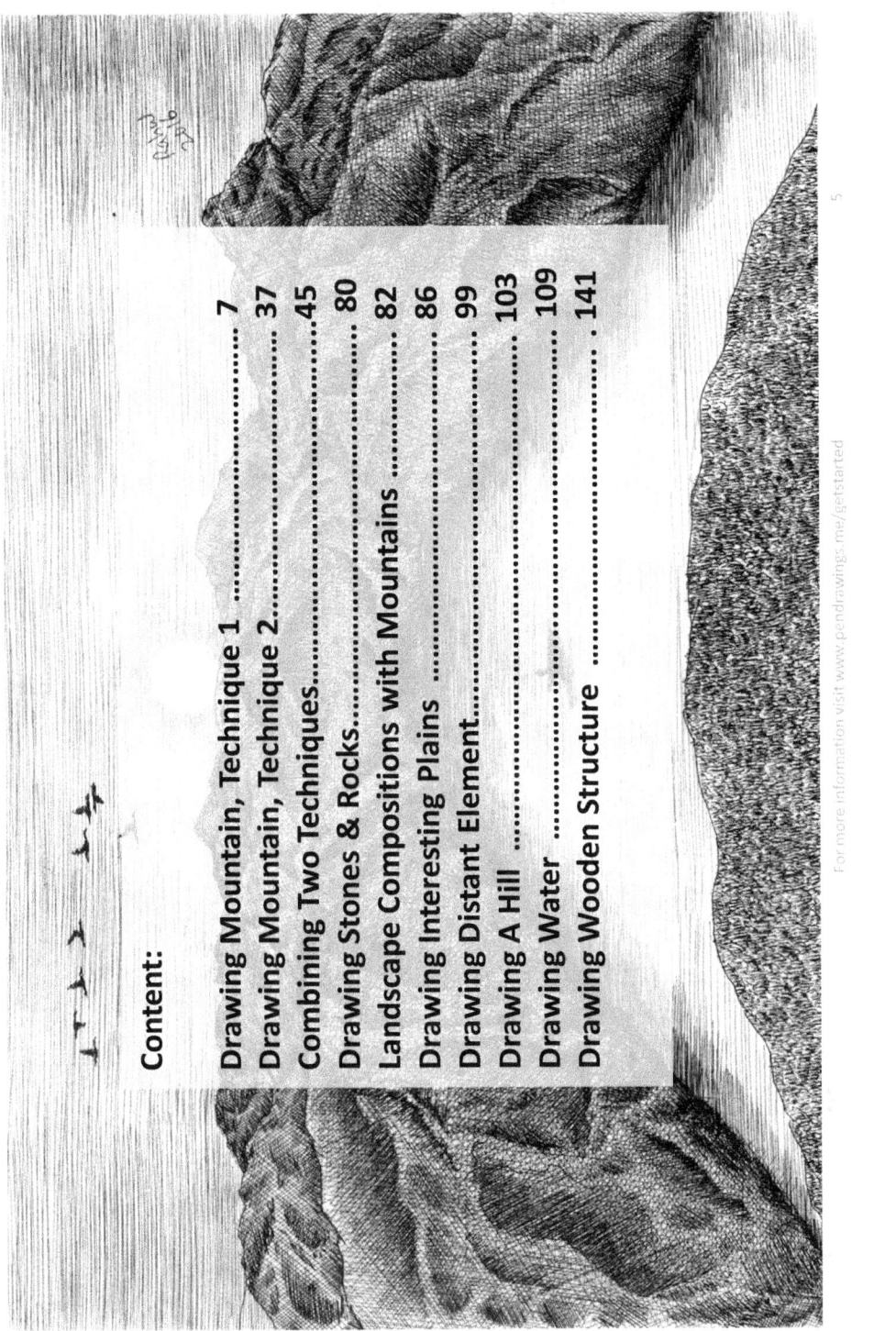

Content:

For more information visit www.pendrawings.me/getstarted

Drawing Mountains:

As you know, mountains come in limitless variety of shapes, sizes and textures. There are 2 primary ways to draw a mountain:

1. **Using different Plains:** In this approach, plains or surfaces at different angles are used to give a feel of mountain.

2. **Using Surface Irregularities:** In this approach crevices and projections from the surface are use to indicate rough texture of mountains.

Here is an example of each approach. In approach 1, angular outline is used to create plains at different angles and textured appropriately. In approach 2, the outline is not angular, instead surface irregularities are used to give feel of mountains.

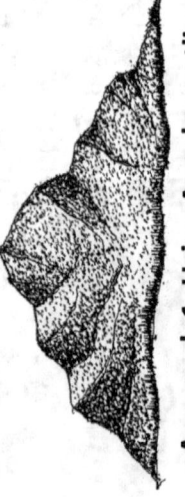

Approach 1, Using Angular outline

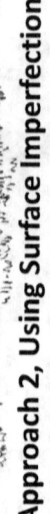

Approach 2, Using Surface Imperfections

There are many variations and use of different strokes in these 2 approaches that we will look at in detail. The two approaches can also be combined to create any kind of mountain from your imagination.

Experiment with different choices and options that are presented in different sections. Once you understand the core techniques, then experiment to see how different choices will affect the outcome. This will help you acquire a deeper understanding and be able to evolve your own style based on your liking.

For more information visit www.pendrawings.me/getstarted

Drawing Mountains with Angular Outline, Approach

We start by looking at a very simple technique to draw pleasing mountains by using just dots and ticks. First step is to draw angular outline and use 'transition points' to define the plains of the mountain. These plains are then brought out by using dots and ticks to texture them appropriately.

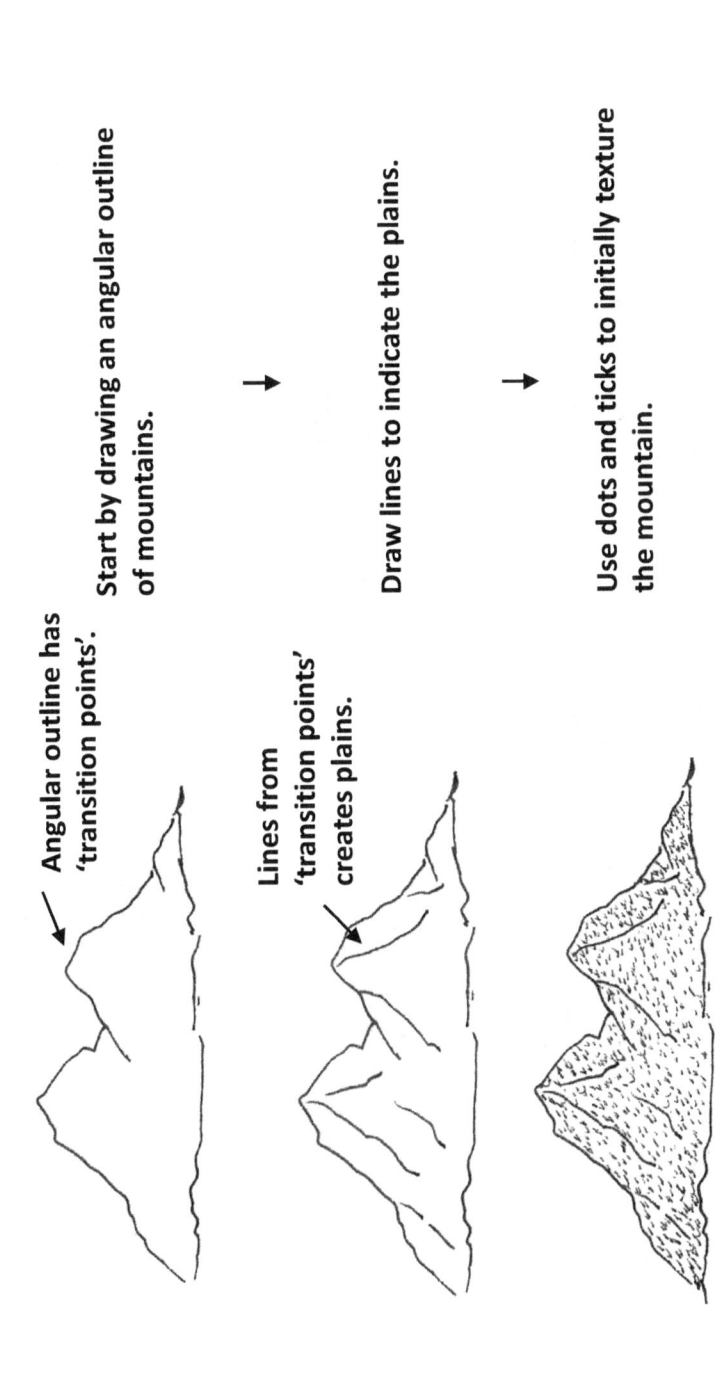

Angular outline has 'transition points'.

Start by drawing an angular outline of mountains.

Lines from 'transition points' creates plains.

Draw lines to indicate the plains.

Use dots and ticks to initially texture the mountain.

Drawing Mountains with Angular Outline, Approach 1, Continued:

Different sides or 'plains' on a mountain will have different tone, or level of darkness. Depending on the direction of light source, sides directly against the light source are darker. Dots are brightly lit while sides away from light sources are darker. This is discussed in detail later. For now, darken the area near plain lines using more dots and ticks.

Use more dots and ticks to add more tone around the plain lines.

Adjust the tone to highlight the plains to your liking. This finishes drawing of mountain.

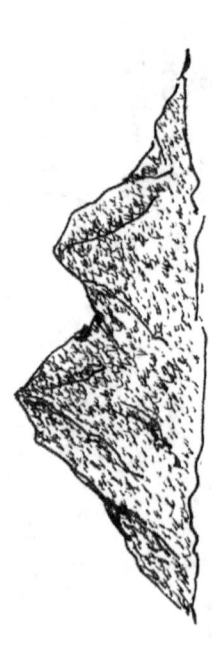

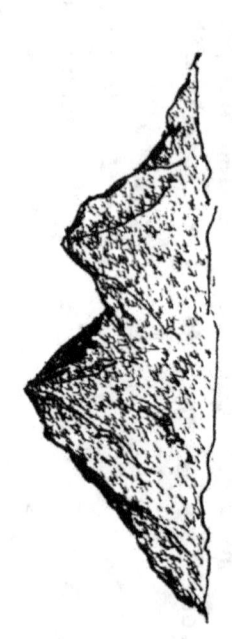

Drawing Angular Outline:

To create plains in the body of the mountain, the outline needs to have distinct change in angle, or a 'transition point'. 'Plain line' drawn from transition points creates the plains as shown below.

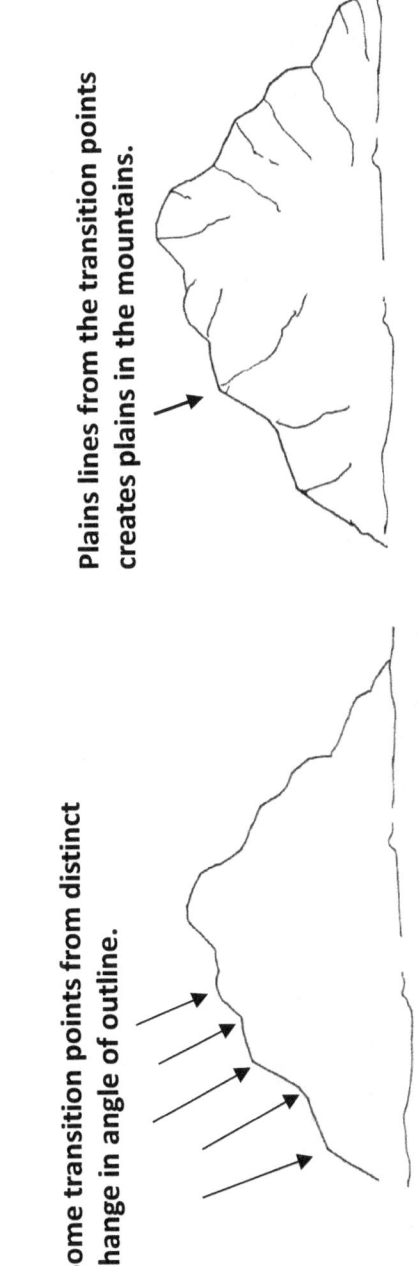

Some transition points from distinct change in angle of outline.

Plains lines from the transition points creates plains in the mountains.

Use interesting angular outline along with irregular and interesting plain lines to create visually pleasing set of plains in the mountain body. Try to keep a balance between the sides.

Some Examples of Outlines:

By using different volume of transition points, very different feel for mountains can be created. Low transition points results in few big plains where as higher volume of transition points creates more plains and more involved mountains.

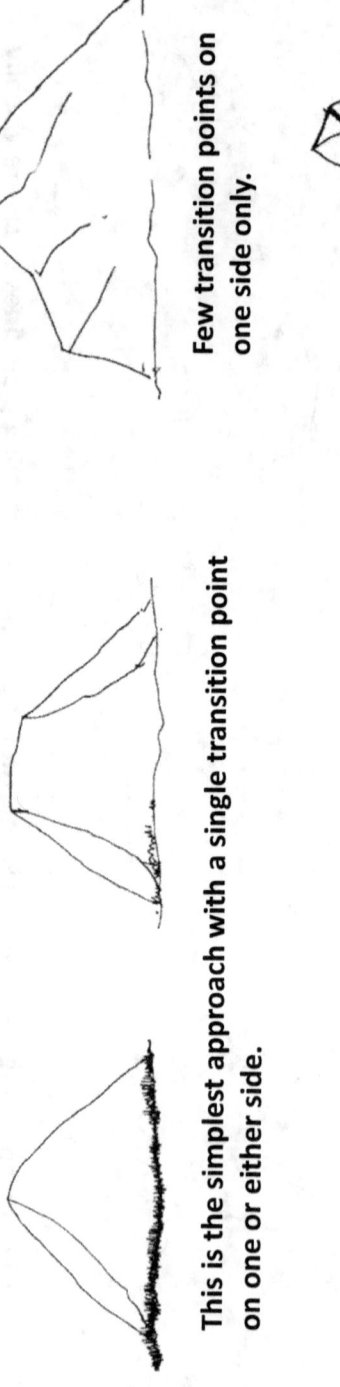

This is the simplest approach with a single transition point on one or either side.

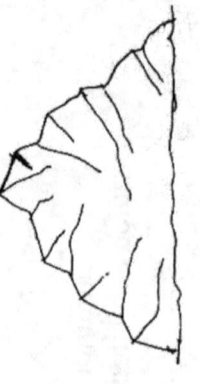

Few transition points on one side only.

A more involved outline.

Distribution of transition points on different sides and height of mountains can be used to create different feel as well.

Activity: Draw Plains in the Following Outlines. Draw some of your own:

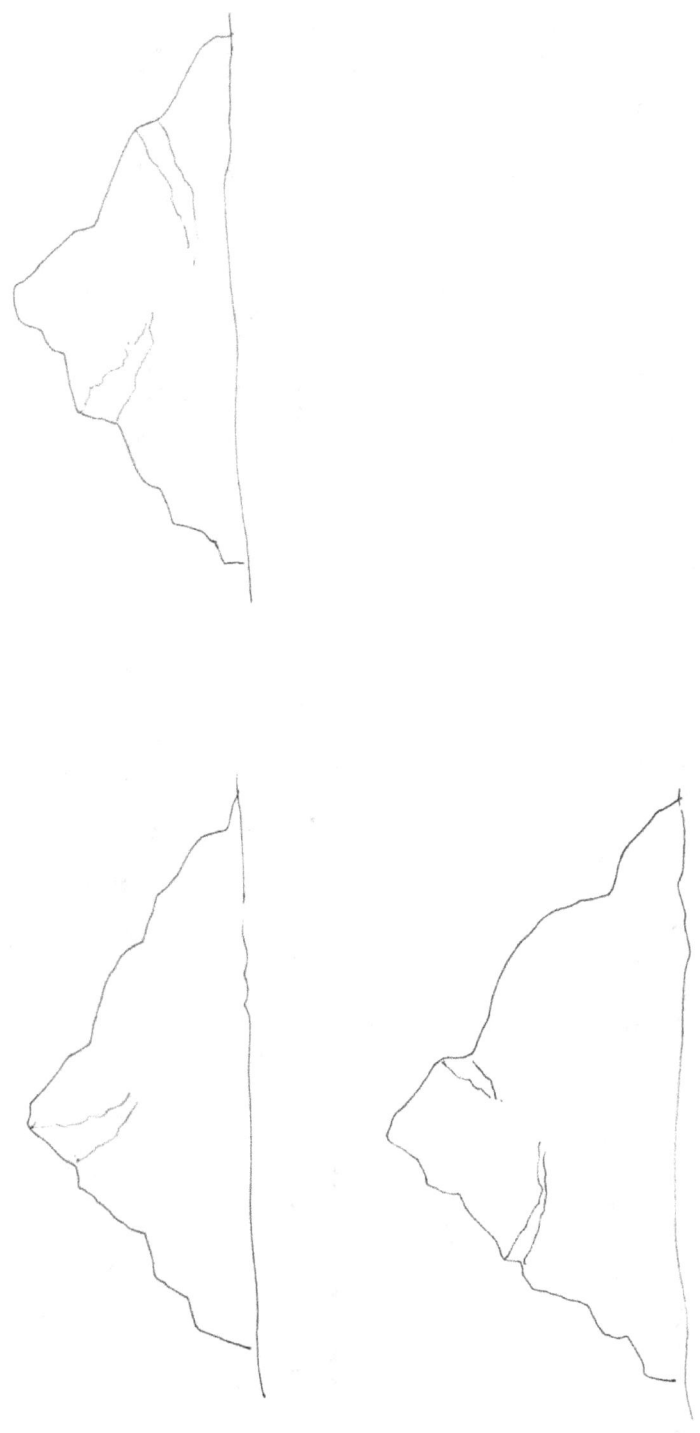

Closed Vs. Open Plains:

Another consideration is how far from the edges should the plains be extended. In one extreme, different plains can be used to fill the entire body of a mountain. This is not usually pleasing. Leave some area in the middle of a mountain 'open', i.e. without explicit indication of plain. Our mind then interprets this area appropriately to give a pleasing indication of mountain.

There is no explicit indication of plains here. Other plains 'merge' in here.

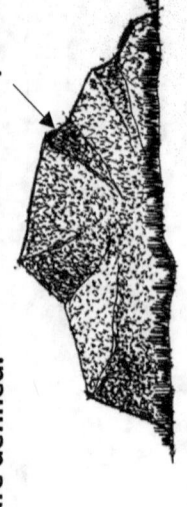

Plains should taper towards the open area.

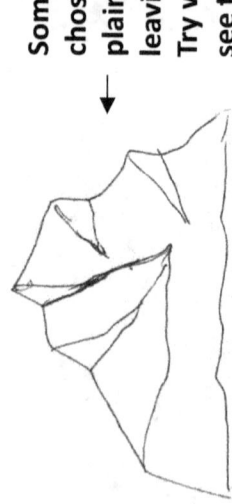

Our mind extends and appropriately interprets the area without plains.

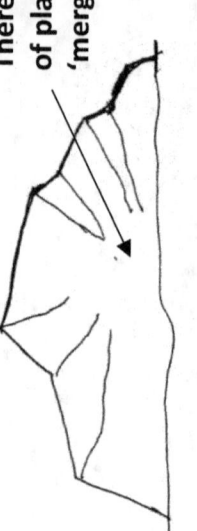

In the same outline, only few open plains from the edges are defined.

Something in between can be chosen as well. Here few plains on the left merge while leaving the other area open. Try with different choices to see the feel you get.

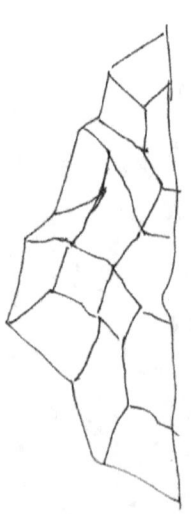

Here Plains are used in all of interior. This is usually not visually appealing.

In the same outline, it is initially very helpful to experiment with drawing different types (open/closed) and sizes of plains. Try it below.

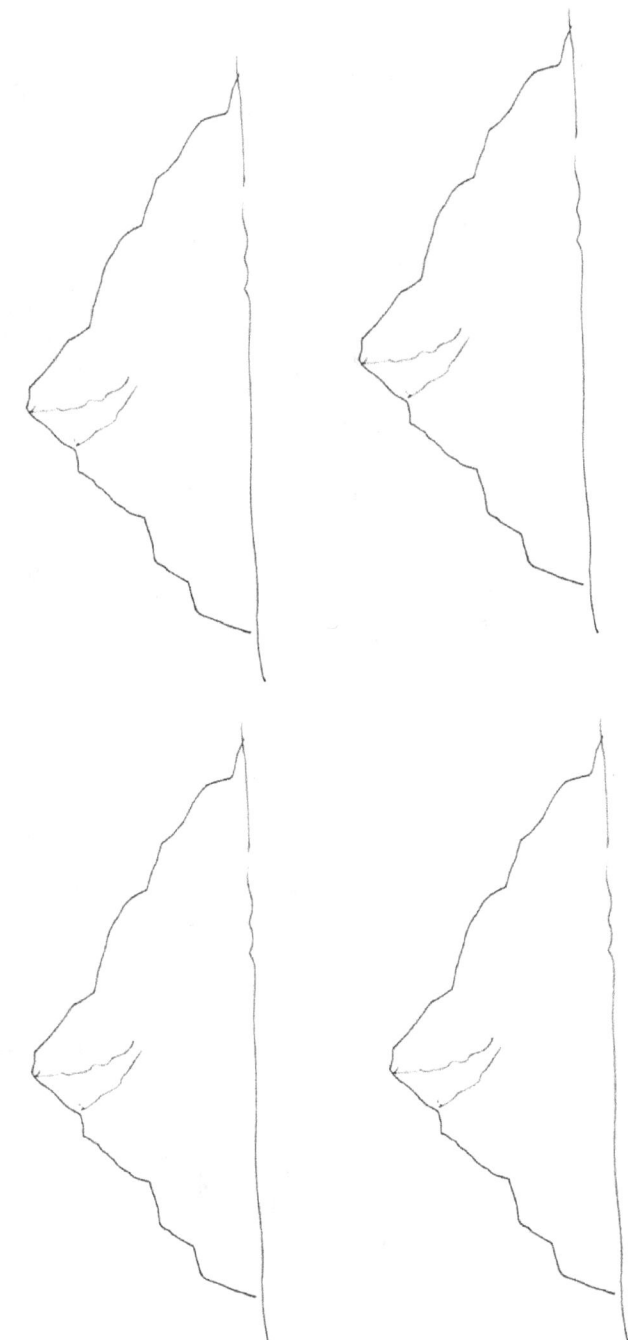

Texturing the Outline:

Start with a uniform base tone using ticks and dots. Next highlight the plains by irregularly adding more tone to the plain lines. Irregularly darken the edges as well.

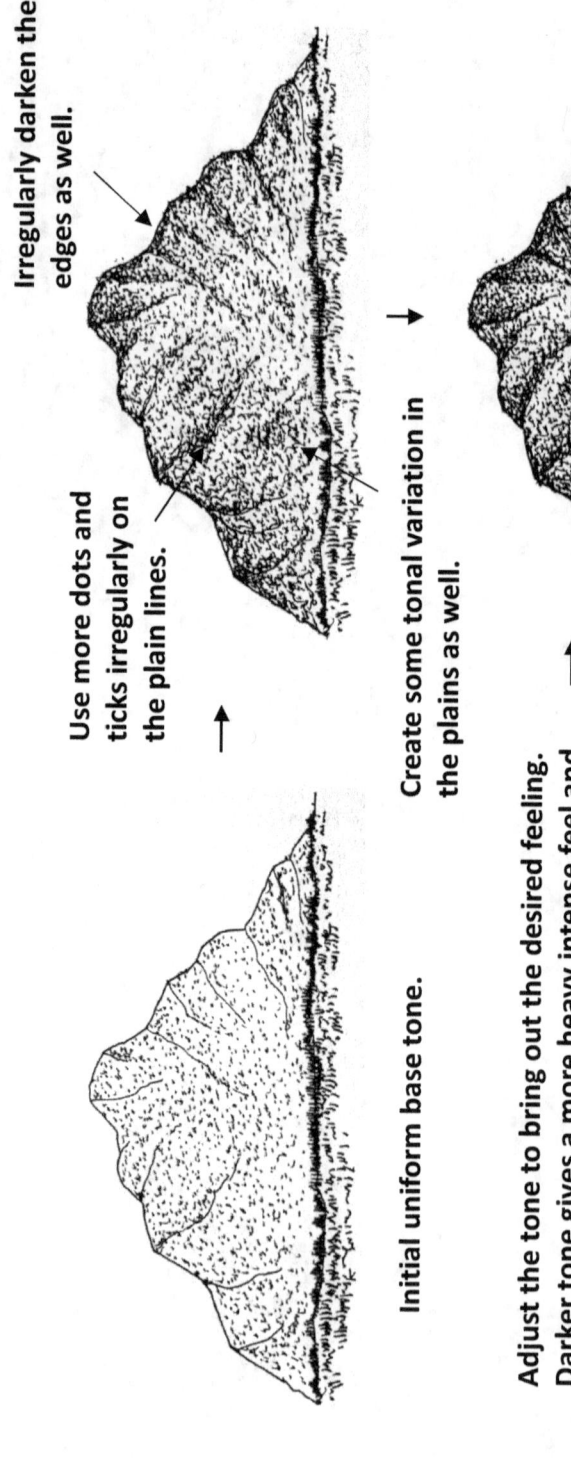

Irregularly darken the edges as well.

Use more dots and ticks irregularly on the plain lines.

Initial uniform base tone.

Create some tonal variation in the plains as well.

Adjust the tone to bring out the desired feeling. Darker tone gives a more heavy intense feel and draws attention to itself.

This is a quick way to texture mountain. More detailed shading is discussed next.

Activity Drawing Mountains, Approach 1:

Texture the following outlines are discussed earlier.

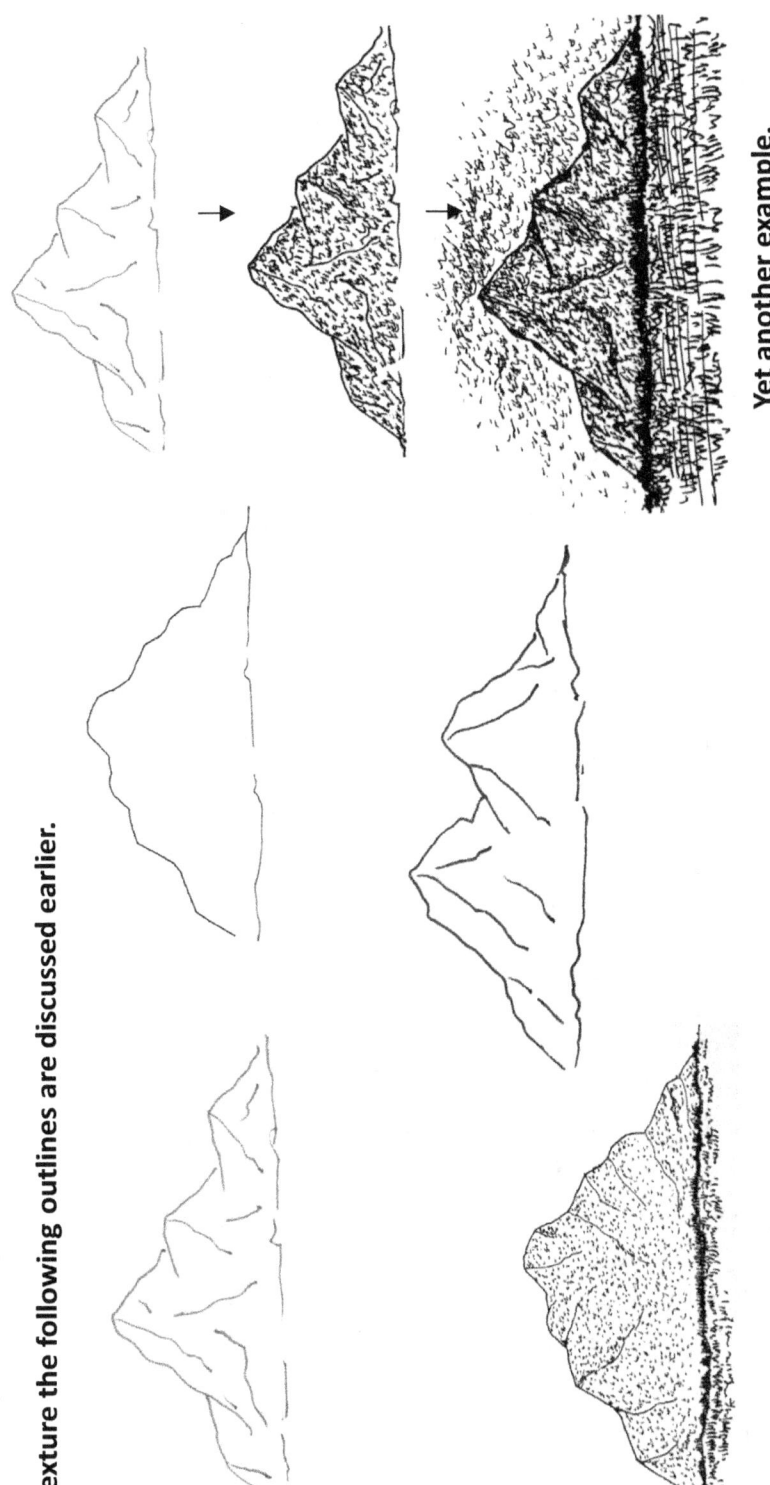

Yet another example.

Finish Texturing.

Concept of Tonal Variation:

Light doesn't fall uniformly on any object which has surfaces at different angle to the light source. For a mountain, the side facing the Sun is brightest and the side away from Sun is darkest. You make an assumption about the direction of Sun and then make the sides of mountain with appropriate tone.

In a typical 3d view, mountain has a 'slice' side. This 'slice' side should be made darker or brighter than other surface depending on where Sun is assumed to be. As the 'slice' is much smaller compared to other surface, it is a good idea to make it darker otherwise the mountain will feel overtly dark.

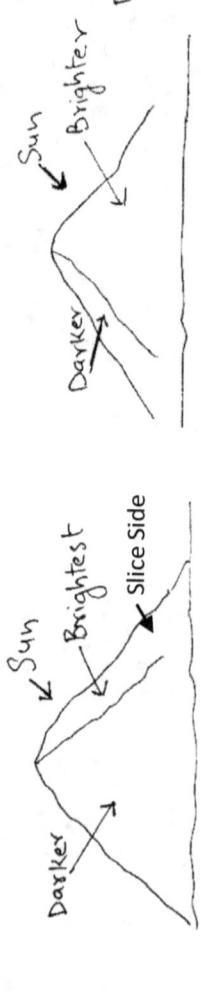

Covering bigger surface with darker tone makes the mountain too dark.

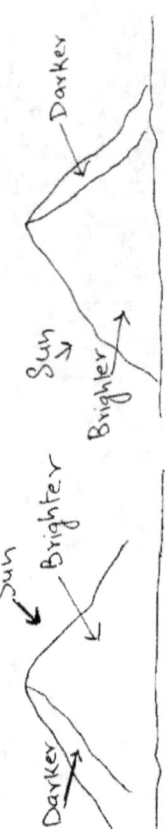

This gives a better feel as darker 'slice' is smaller in size

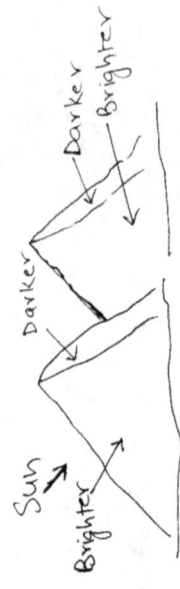

Keep it consistent across mountains

Shading Mountains with Tonal Variation:

It is very important to understand the concept discussed on last page. If two plains of a mountain are at different angle to the viewer, then they need to have different tones to indicate that. This is shown step by step in next few pages. We start with very simple mountains with slice on either side.

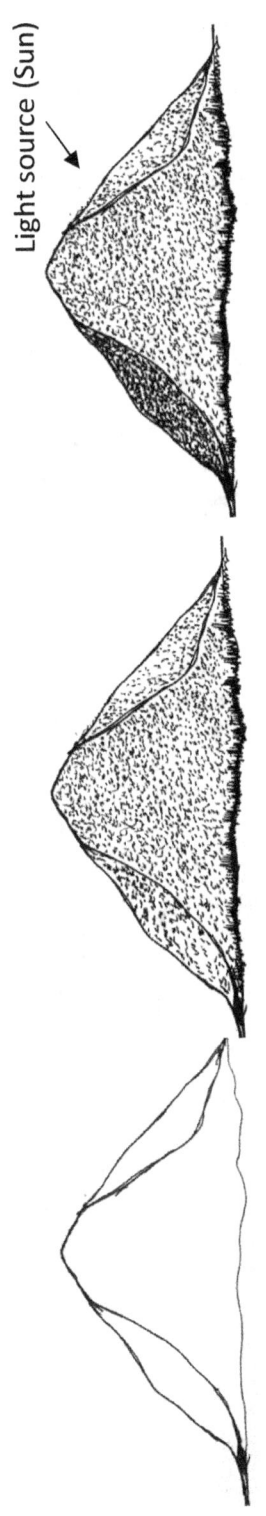

Light source (Sun)

We start with a simple outline with 2 opposing faces to illustrate aspects of shading.

Principle of Shading:
Faces towards the light source are lit brighter (less tone) than faces angling away from light source (more darker, more tone).

Initially a uniform tone is given. This doesn't bring out the form and the mountain looks flat.

Next we assume a light source and based on that determine which face will be lit more. With assumed light source from right, left 'slice' will have lot less light and is shaded darker. This difference in tone between the left and right face gives feeling of form to the mountain.

Shading Mountains, Continued:

Level of tonal variation or shading to add depends on the size of the drawing and the feel you intend to give to the drawing. With smaller drawings, the faces might be very small in size and often it is difficult to add subtle tonal variation to small size faces. This is discussed further later. Also sometimes more tonal contrast can be used to give more dramatic feel to the mountain.

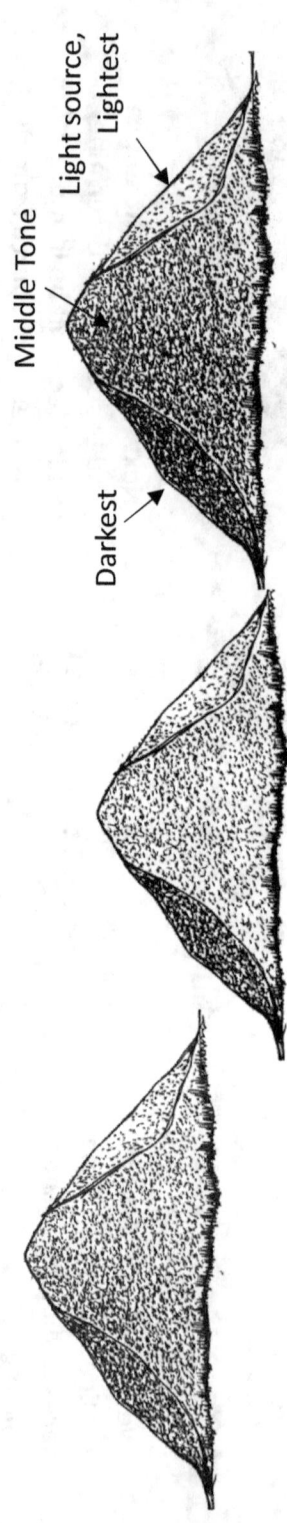

Light source, Lightest

Middle Tone

Darkest

In comparing these 2 drawings, left one has subtle tonal variations with less intensity on the left face. Right one has more dramatic transition with darker tone on the left face. Such choices gives different feel to the drawing.

Principle of Shading:

Choose the level of shading and transition between tones based on the feel you intend to achieve.

Level of shading detail: In the drawing above I have further created tonal transition across the viewer facing face with darker tones on side away from the light source. This gives a bit more 'realism' but decreases the level of tonal contrast between adjacent faces and hence makes it less dramatic and 'attention seeking' compared to drawing on left

Shading Mountains, Continued:

Slice in a mountain also usually has depth. To bring out depth, different tone can be used on slice to indicate that. Add a 'tapered dark' as shown below to add depth to the slice. This also helps to establish visual contrast with other mountains behind it as we will see next.

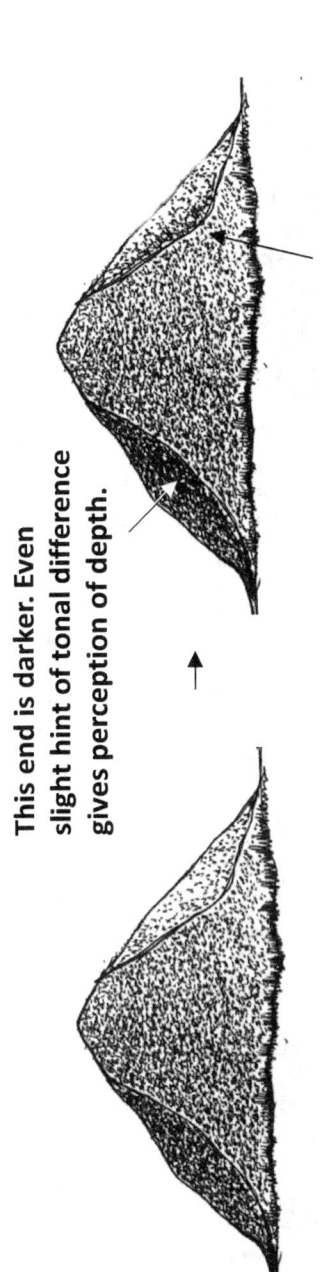

This end is darker. Even slight hint of tonal difference gives perception of depth.

Add slight tone in a tapered manner to slice helps to give it depth and more visual interest. This can be done for both slices.

Shading Mountain Range:

In a mountain range with receding mountains, use the same direction of light to shade individual mountains.

Lighter top of slice contrasts with darker tone of behind mountain and creates separation between the two.

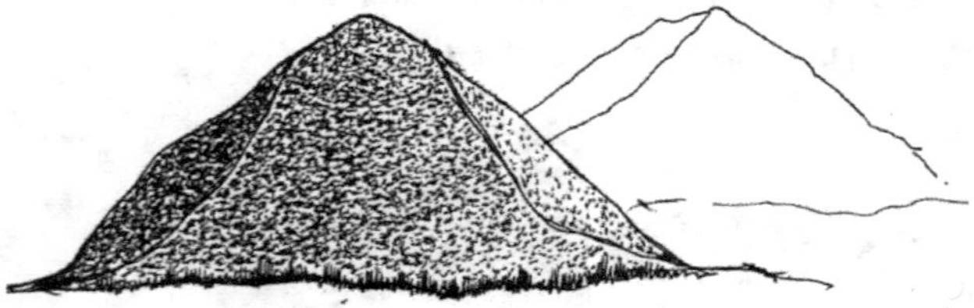

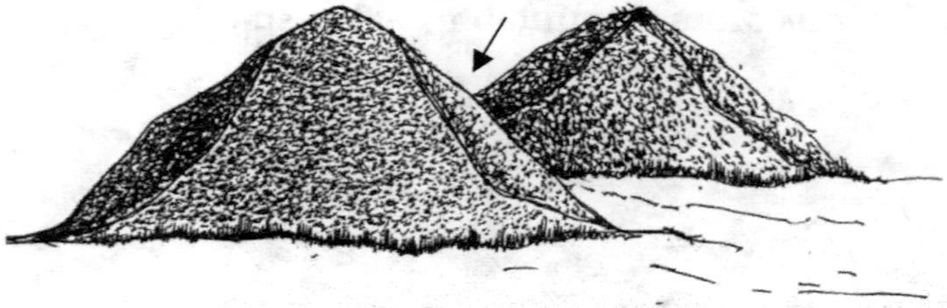

Draw smaller receding mountains as shown above.

Use same direction of light to shade behind mountain.

Texture the following outlines with tonal variation to bring out their form as discussed earlier.

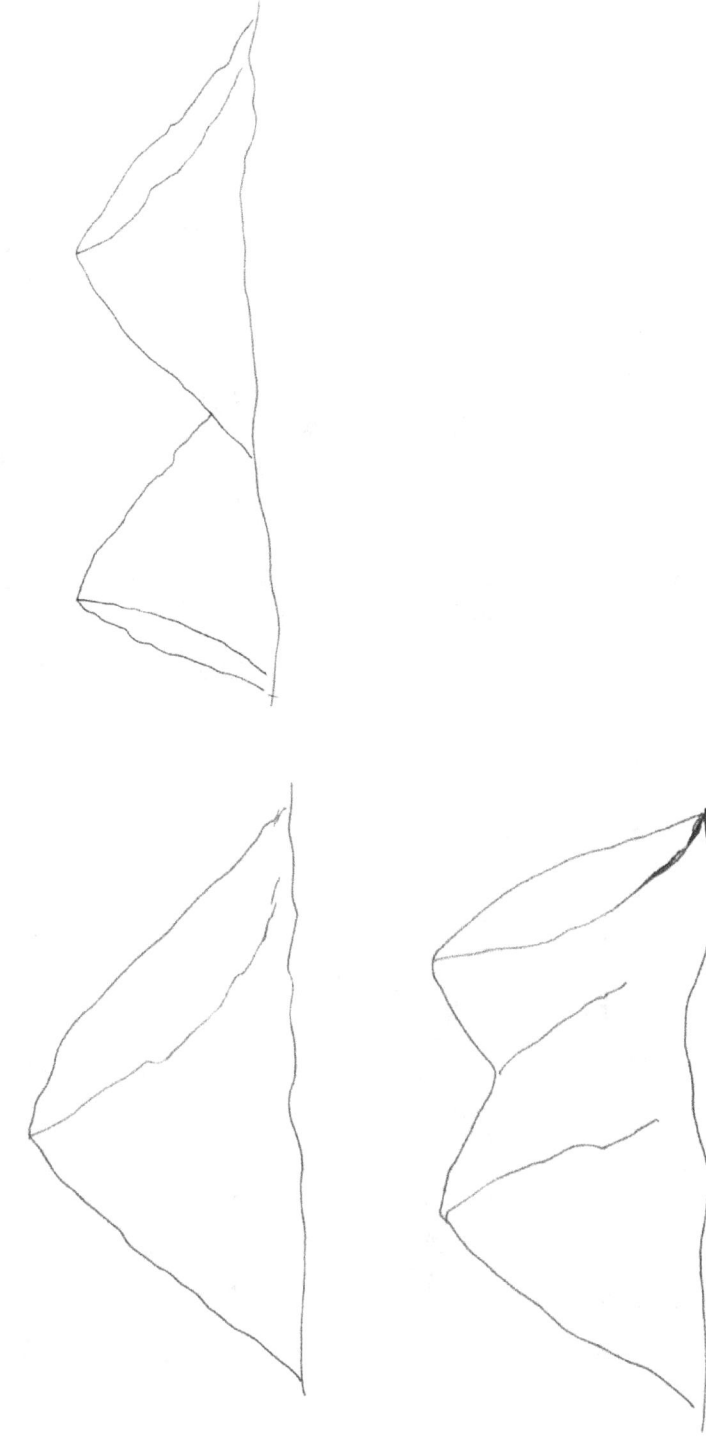

Keep Mountains Distinct:

It is very important to keep mountains visually distinct to keep their appearance visually pleasing. In the absence of color, it can be done either with tonal contrast, or if the tone is similar to adjacent sides, then leave a small sliver of white to maintain separation.

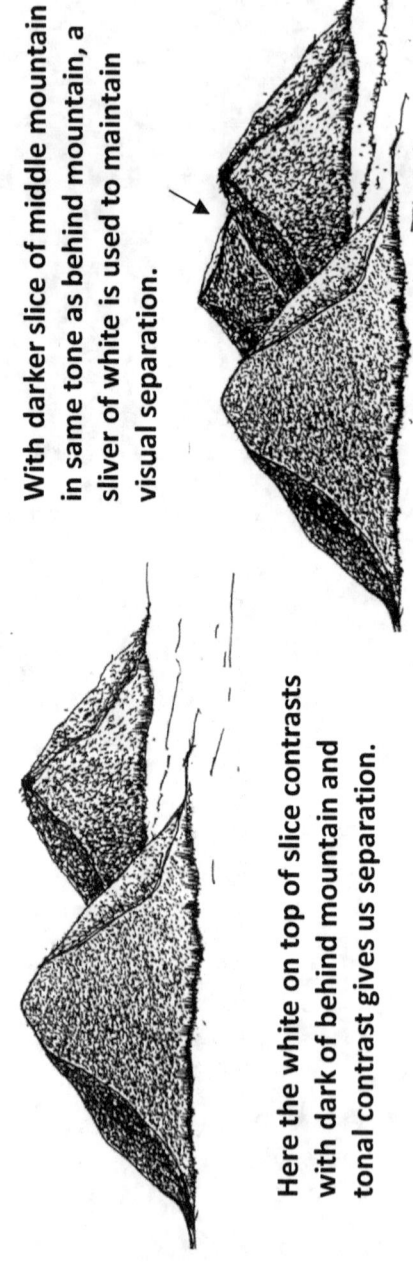

With darker slice of middle mountain in same tone as behind mountain, a sliver of white is used to maintain visual separation.

Here the white on top of slice contrasts with dark of behind mountain and tonal contrast gives us separation.

Here a small layer of white is used to maintain separation between the back and middle mountain. This small sliver is ignored by our mind when viewing. Keep it very small.

Always maintain visual separation between different elements by using different tone levels or leaving a streak of white between them.

Concept of Tonal Variation Extended to More Involved Outline:

When a mountain with many angular plains is drawn, same concept of tonal difference between plains at different angle to each other need to be observed. Depending on the light source, same plain can be lighter or dark, but it should always have a different tone compared to plain at a different angle.

This plain is slightly at different angle than plain 1 and hence they should have slight difference in tone but not too much.

These 2 plains are at different angle and hence need to have different tone.

These two plain are at same angle to viewer and hence can have similar tone.

Plain 1

Shading Mountains, Continued:

A very common theme is to draw mountains with alternating horizontal and vertical faces as shown below. In this case, as discussed on last page, assume a direction of light source with vertical faces towards the light source having lighter tone and vertical faces away from the light source the darkest. Horizontal faces are toned in between.

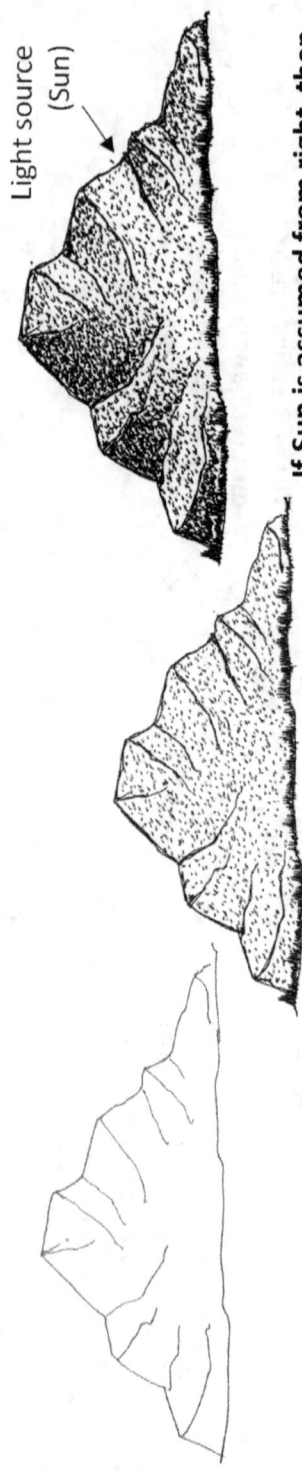

Light source (Sun)

A typical mountain with alternating vertical and horizontal faces. Depending on the direction of light source, different faces will have different tones.

If Sun is assumed from right, then vertical faces directly towards Sun are lightest (less tone). Vertical faces on the other side are darkest. Horizontal faces on right will be lighter than horizontal faces on left but such tonal difference can't be textured at this size.

Principle of Shading:

Goal is to bring out the desired feel for Form and Volume. Use the level of shading that does it. Don't over do it.

Shading Mountains, Continued:

One pleasing approach to shading is to assuming light source/Sun from Top and make vertical sides darker and horizontal plains lighter. This manner of shading is usually visually pleasing.

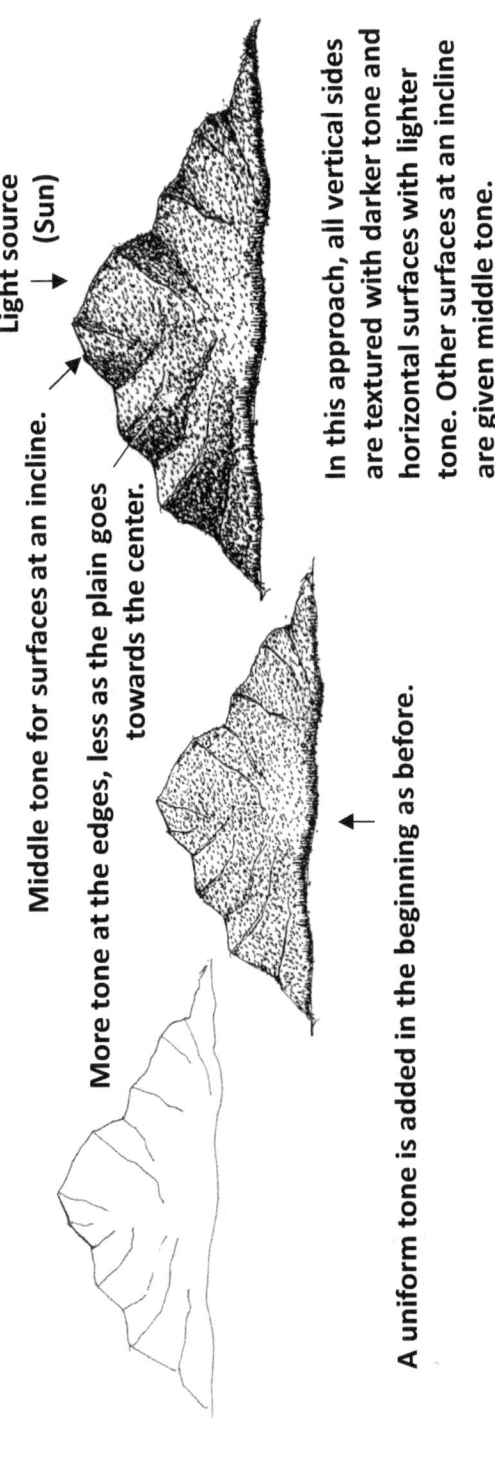

Light source
→ (Sun)

Middle tone for surfaces at an incline.

More tone at the edges, less as the plain goes towards the center.

In this approach, all vertical sides are textured with darker tone and horizontal surfaces with lighter tone. Other surfaces at an incline are given middle tone.

A uniform tone is added in the beginning as before.

This approach is easy to do and produces visually pleasing result. This shading is used in remaining examples in this book.

Drawing a Mountain Range:

A mountain range is usually visually more pleasing than a single mountain. To draw a range, draw successive mountains behind as shown below. Make them progressively smaller as they go out.

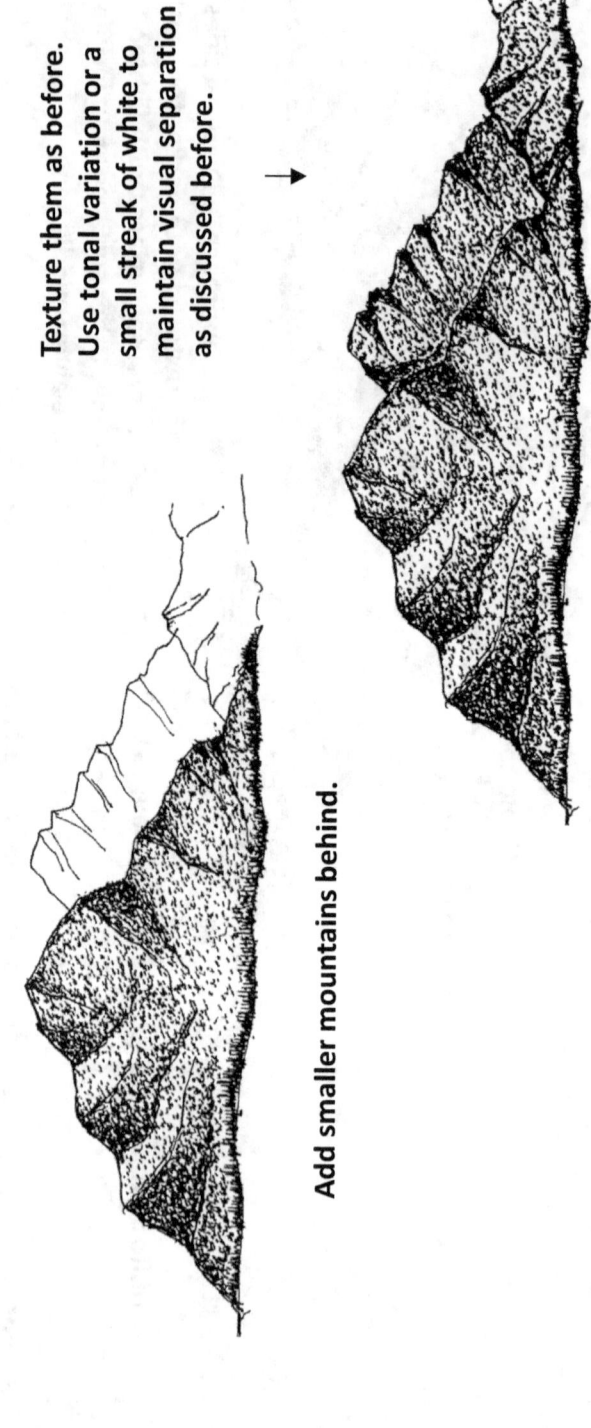

Add smaller mountains behind.

Texture them as before. Use tonal variation or a small streak of white to maintain visual separation as discussed before.

Activity: Texturing More Angular Outline:

Texture the following outlines based on shown direction of light as discussed previously.

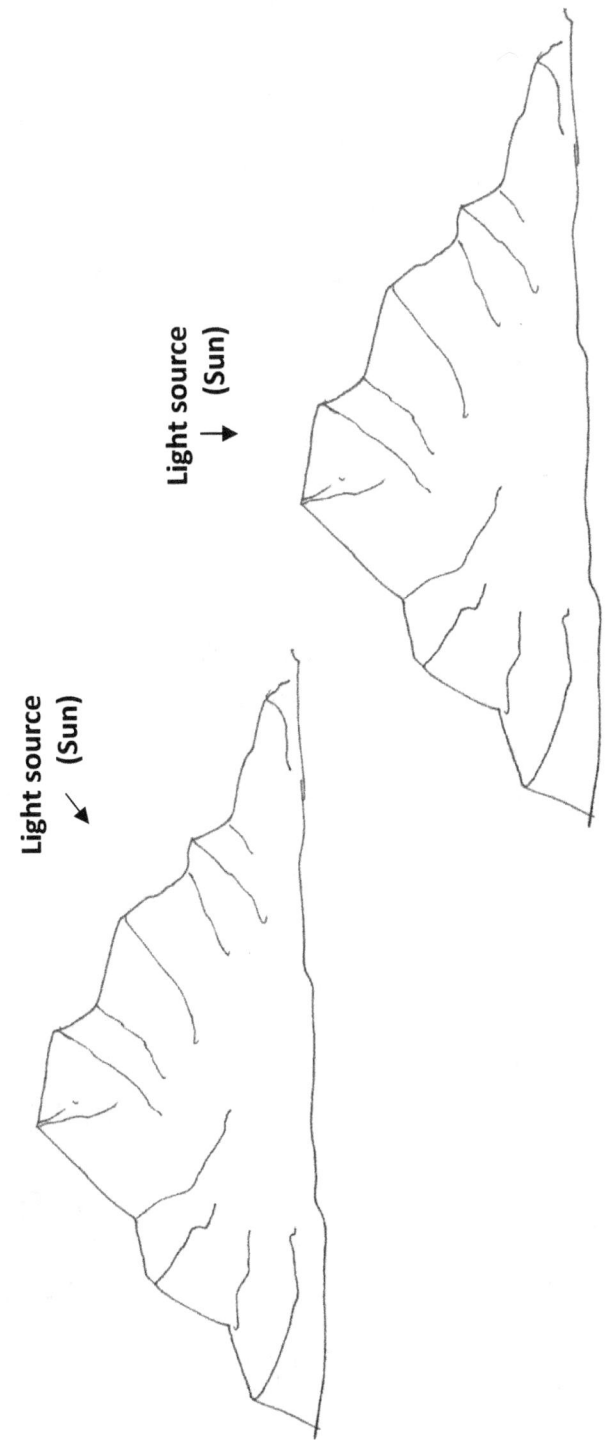

Light source
(Sun)

Light source
(Sun)

A Simpler Approach to Shading:

We discussed shading in detail in last few pages. This is more involved shading with different sides given tones in accordance with the light they would receive. Another simpler approach is to darken the plain line and edges irregularly as seen in step by step example before. This still brings out the dimensionality of mountain and is especially useful if mountain is drawn smaller in size and full shading is difficult to do.

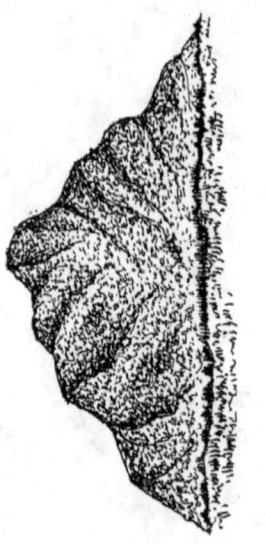

Here is another example we saw before. By irregularly darkening plain lines, feeling of volume is established.

For a smaller size, irregularly darken the plain lines as shown. This helps to distinguish the plains and brings out the form. This is usually enough to give volume to the mountain.

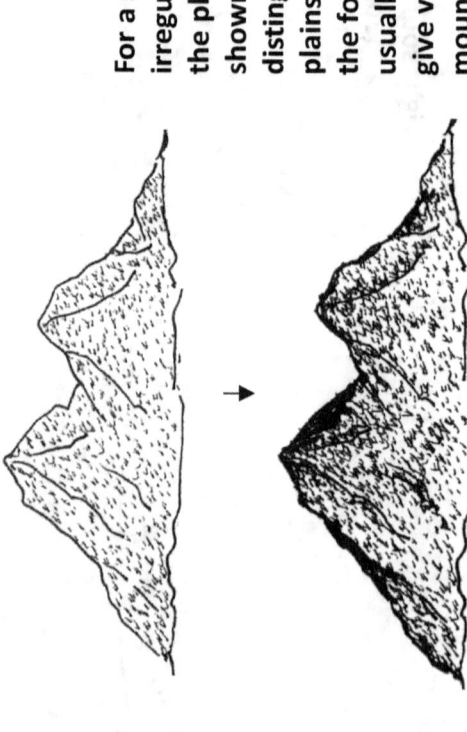

This approach was used in drawing mountain in the beginning.

Use Appropriate Shading Level:

There needs to be tonal difference between plains at different angles but you can experiment with level of such tonal difference. More contrast between plains brings out dimensionality more but also increases the overall tone level.

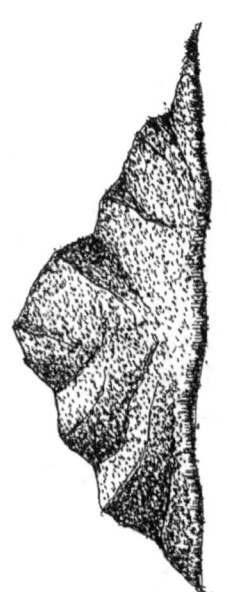

Use of more tonal levels, gives more form but also raises the overall tone level and makes mountain seek attention.

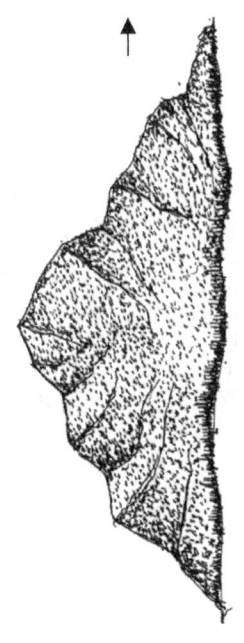

Here only slight tonal difference is used. This still gives a sense of form. If you don't want mountains to draw attention in your drawing, then this level might be enough.

Use the level of shading that is permissible by the size of the drawing and is in line with your overall drawing. If you want mountains to be focal points and seek attention, then make then darker with more tonal variations in shading. Otherwise, lighter approach as shown can be used.

Level of Detail:

When drawing mountains with many small plains, like below, depending on size, you might not be able to do full shading. In this case use the approach to highlighting plain lines.

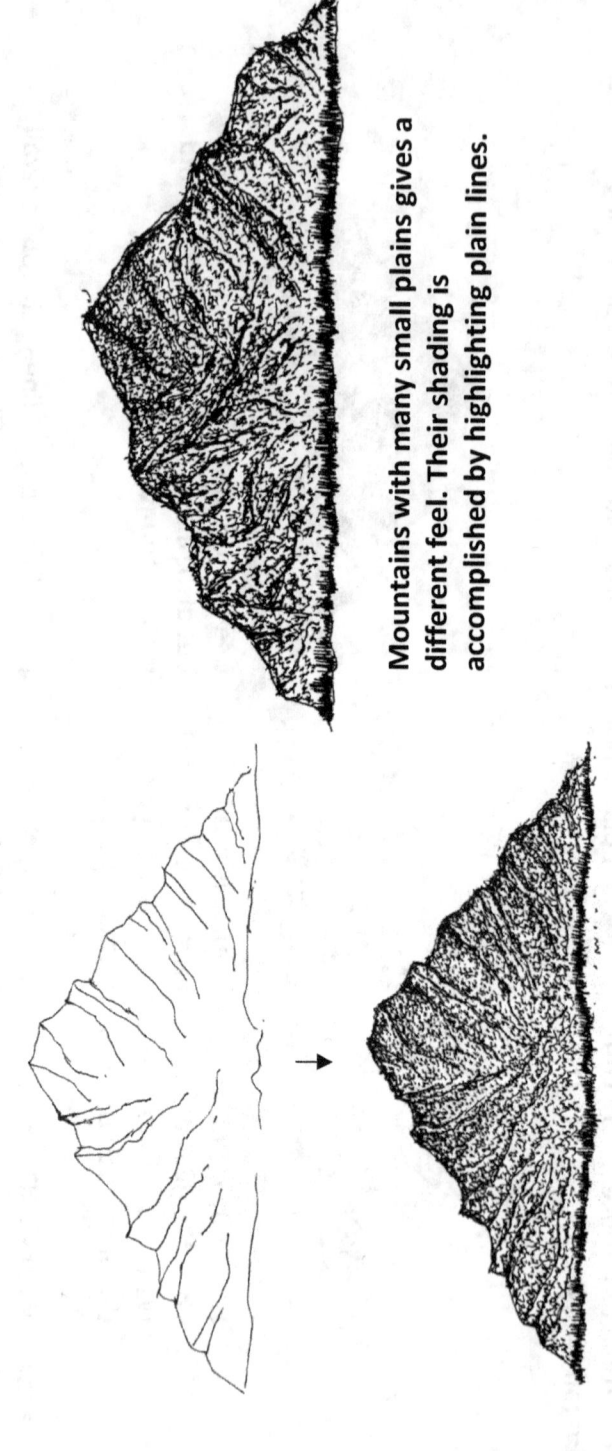

Mountains with many small plains gives a different feel. Their shading is accomplished by highlighting plain lines.

Activity: Texturing outline with more detail:

In the same following outlines, use different levels of shading based on previous discussion to see the effect you get. Start with highlighting plain lines and successively add more tone.

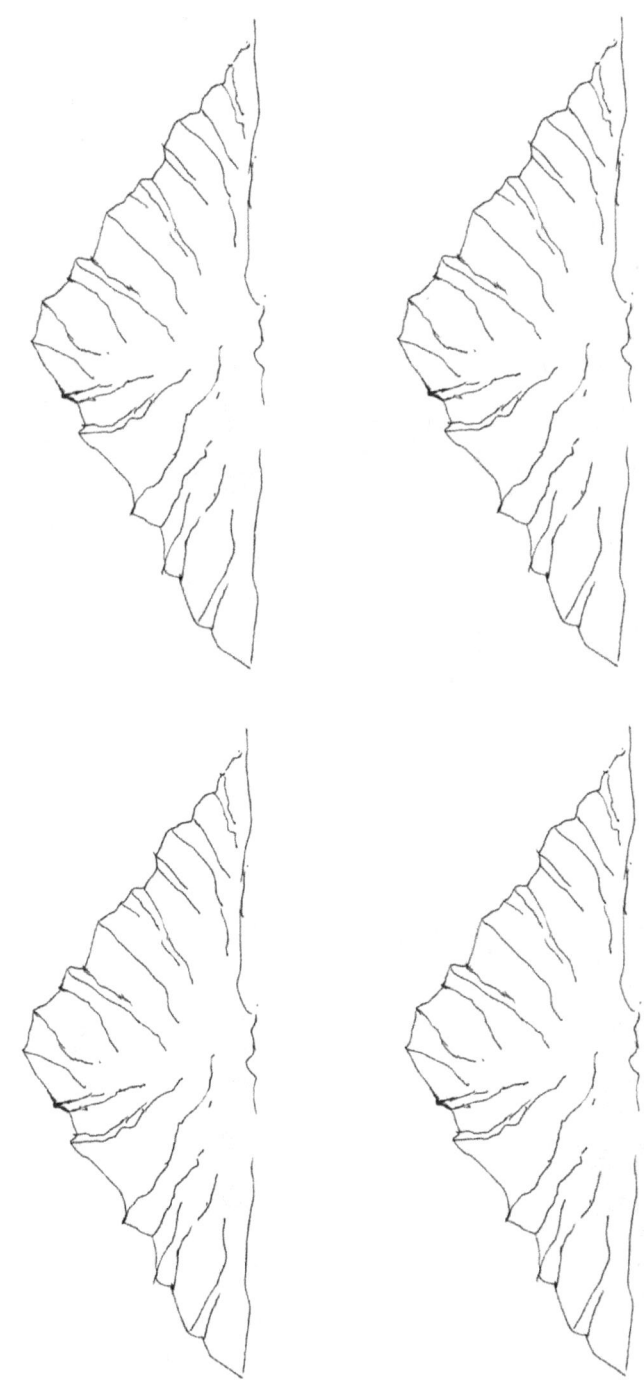

Using Parallel Lines to Shade Mountains:

Parallel lines are another option to texture mountains. This gives a different feel compared to use of dots and ticks as seen below.

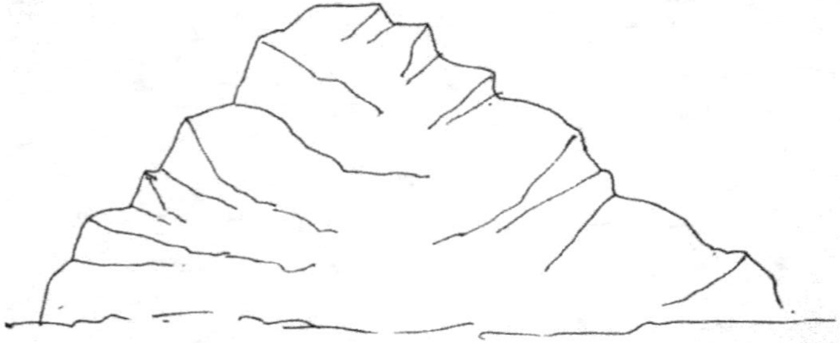

Angle of parallel lines is along the angle of plain. This brings out the orientation of the plain.

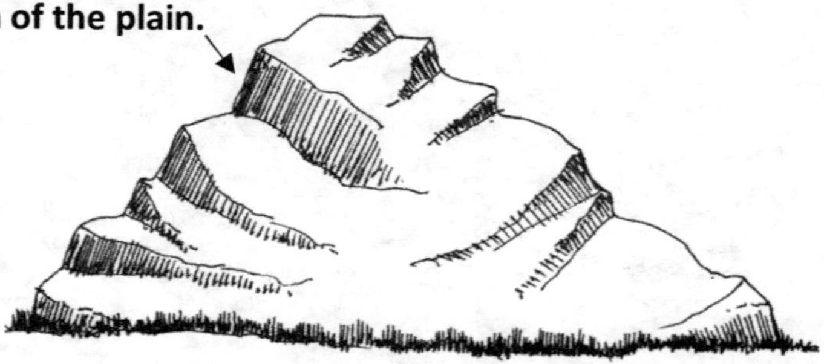

For shading, use parallel lines oriented along the angle of vertically oriented plains.

Start with an outline as before.

Using Parallel Lines to Shade Mountains, Continued:

Dots and ticks gives a bit coarser feel compared to use of fine parallel lines. Both can be used to texture mountains in different settings to add varied interest to the drawing.

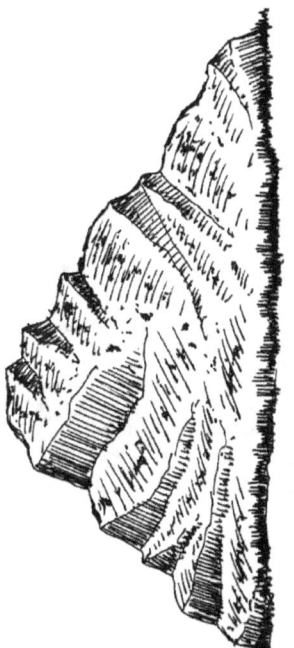

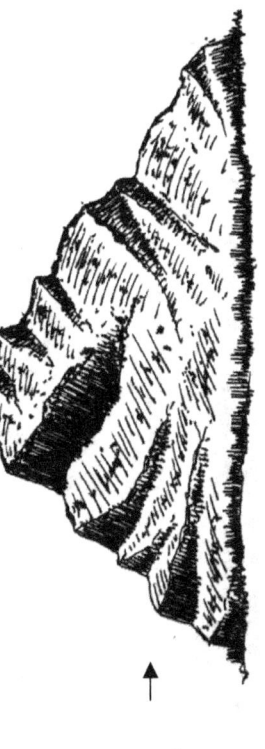

Use small ticks and tapered crevices to add roughness to the surface.

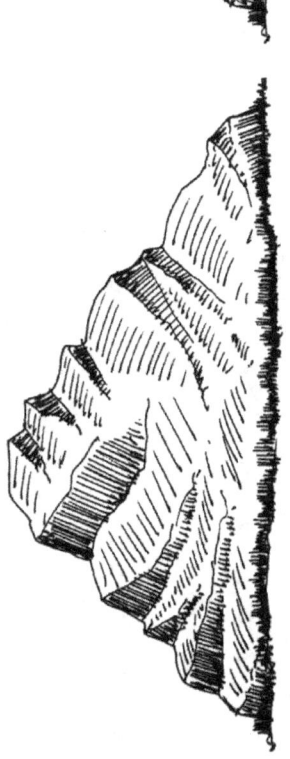

For horizontally oriented surfaces, used parallel lines to give surface contours as shown.

To further bring out contrast, vertically oriented sides can be further darkened.

Using Right Direction of Parallel Lines:

When using parallel lines for sides, they should be used in appropriate direction to bring out the feel for the sides. This is referred to as 'Directional Hatching' where direction of lines also indicates the orientation of the plain. Similarly, surface contour lines for horizontally oriented surfaces should be along that direction.

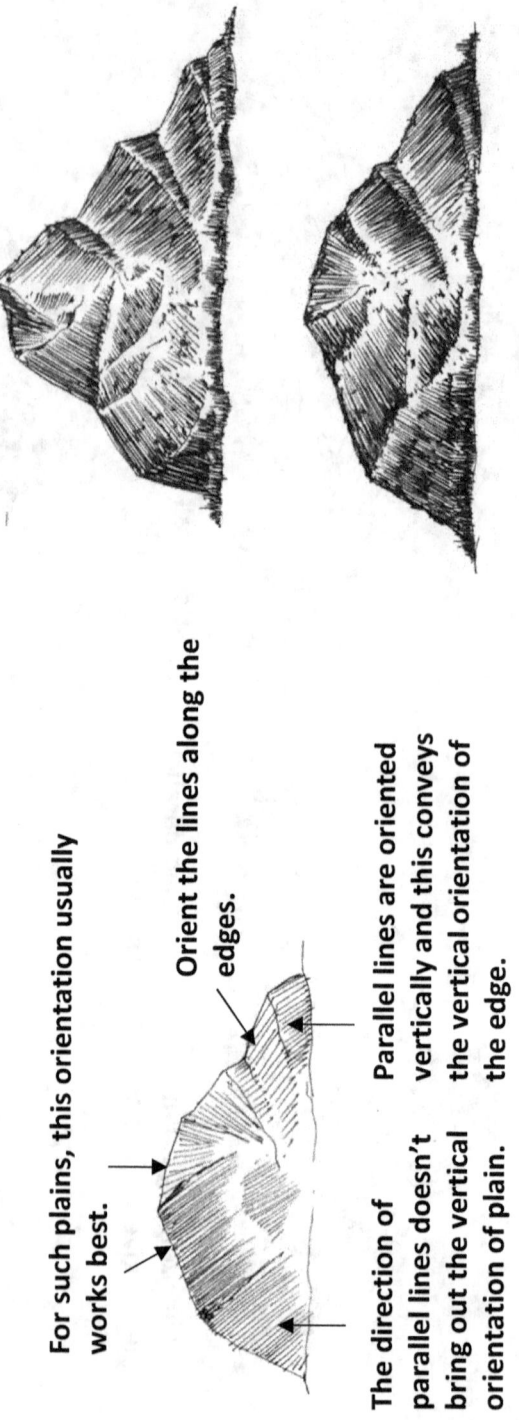

For such plains, this orientation usually works best.

Orient the lines along the edges.

The direction of parallel lines doesn't bring out the vertical orientation of plain.

Parallel lines are oriented vertically and this conveys the vertical orientation of the edge.

Some more examples.

Activity: Texturing Mountain with Parallel Lines:

Texture the following outlines with parallel lines. Drawing parallel lines (hatching) using pen takes practice. If you are not proficient in it, use this as a practice to improve as this is a fundamental part of drawing with pen.

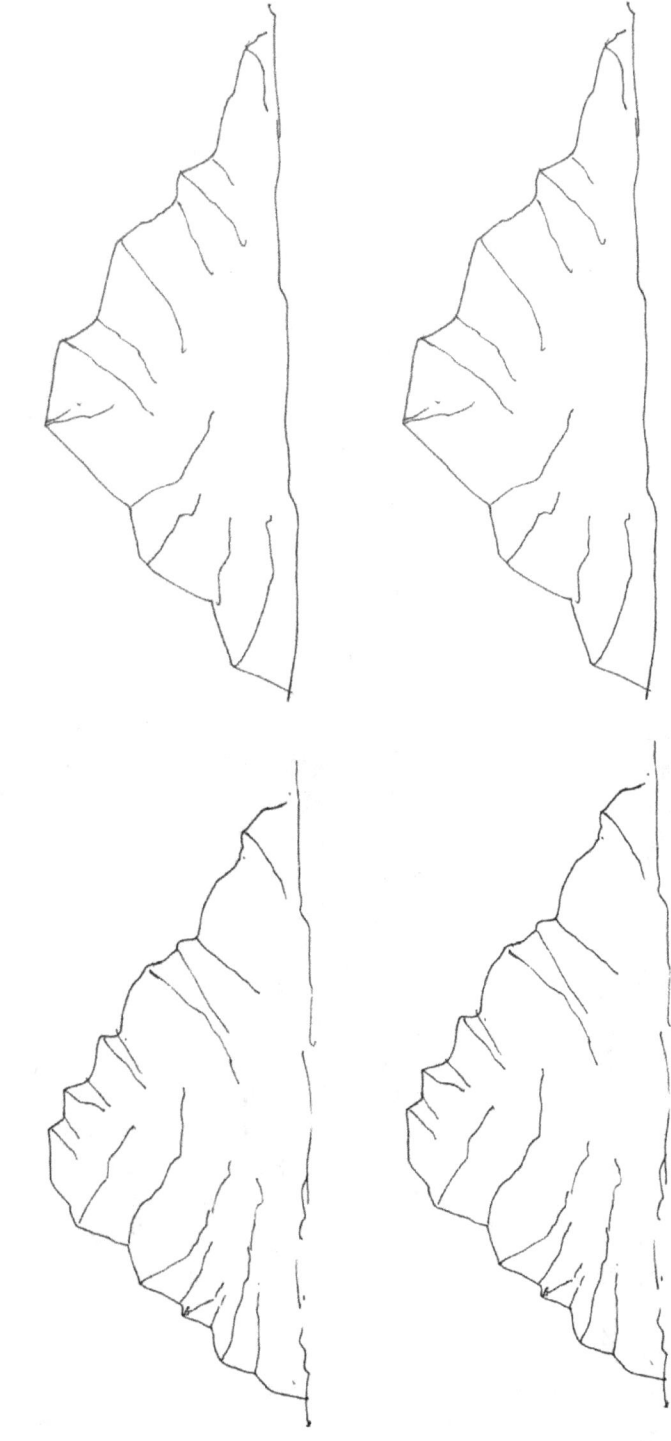

Yet More Examples:

Here are some more examples. Different choices for the size, orientation and interplay of different plains give very different feel to the mountains.

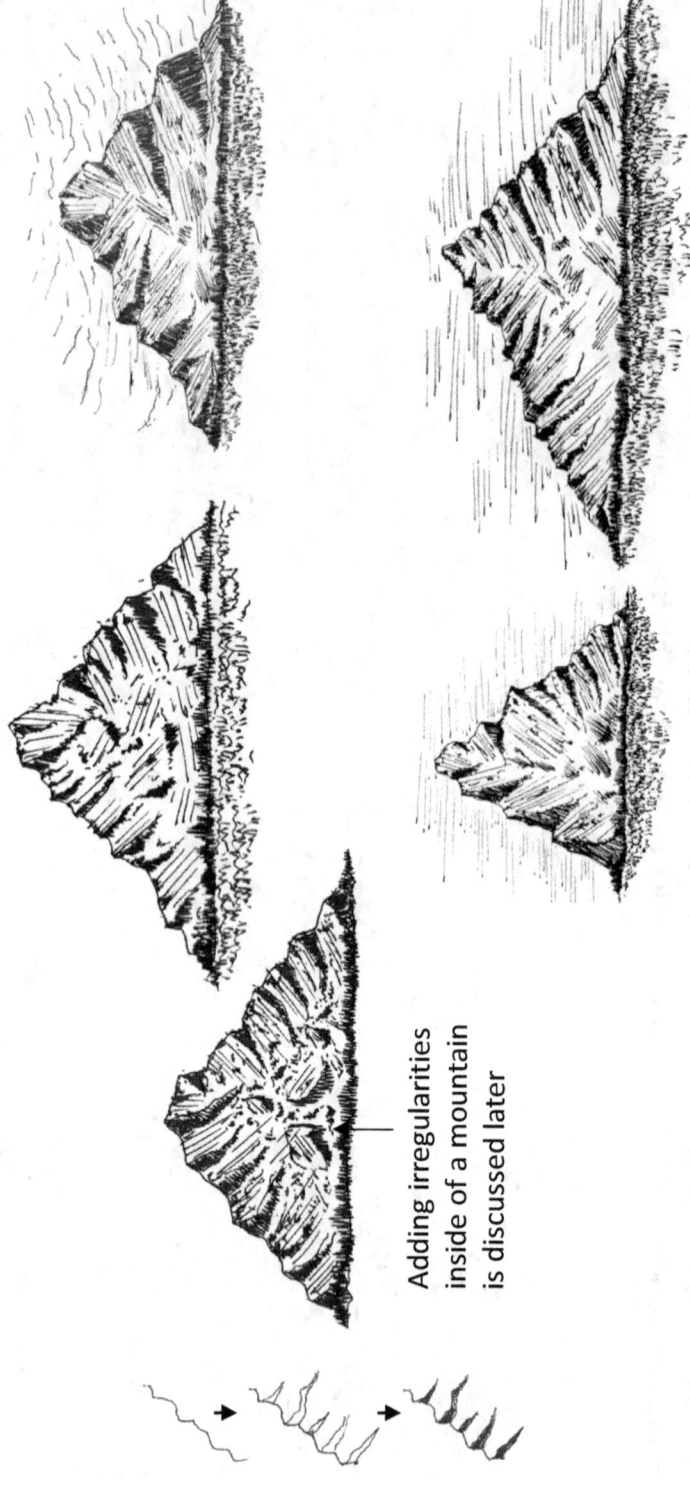

Adding irregularities inside of a mountain is discussed later

For more information visit www.pendrawings.me/getstarted

Drawing Mountains with Surface Imperfections, Approach 2:

Next we look at how to draw mountains by indicating surface imperfections. In the earlier approach, focus was on defining angled plains from edges that gave an impression of mountain. In approach 2, we will learn how to indicate irregularities on the surface to give a pleasing feel of mountain.

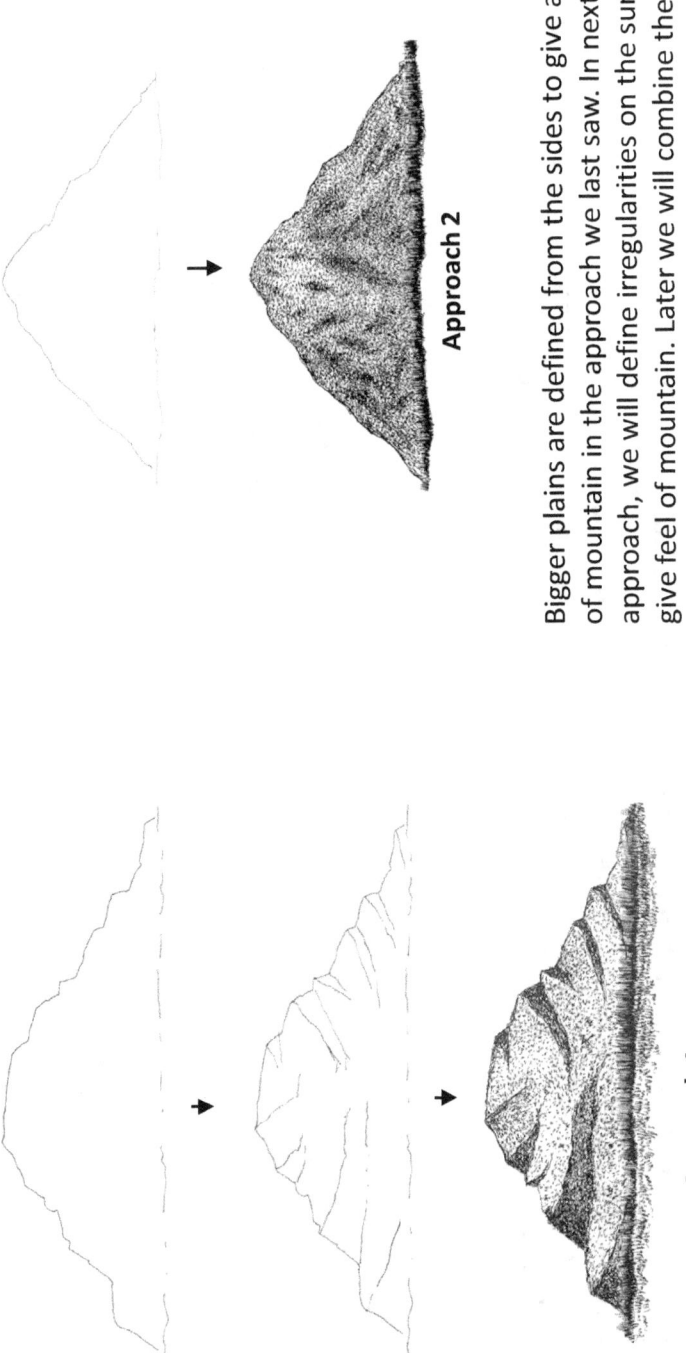

Approach 2

Approach 1

Bigger plains are defined from the sides to give a feeling of mountain in the approach we last saw. In next approach, we will define irregularities on the surface to give feel of mountain. Later we will combine the two.

Drawing Mountains with Surface Imperfections, Indicating a Cut:

A surface cut is indicated with a tapered dark shape as shown below. The plain of cut is at a different angle to the surrounding surface and hence less light reaches the cut plain. Tapered shape and darker tone conveys a feel of surface cut to our mind.

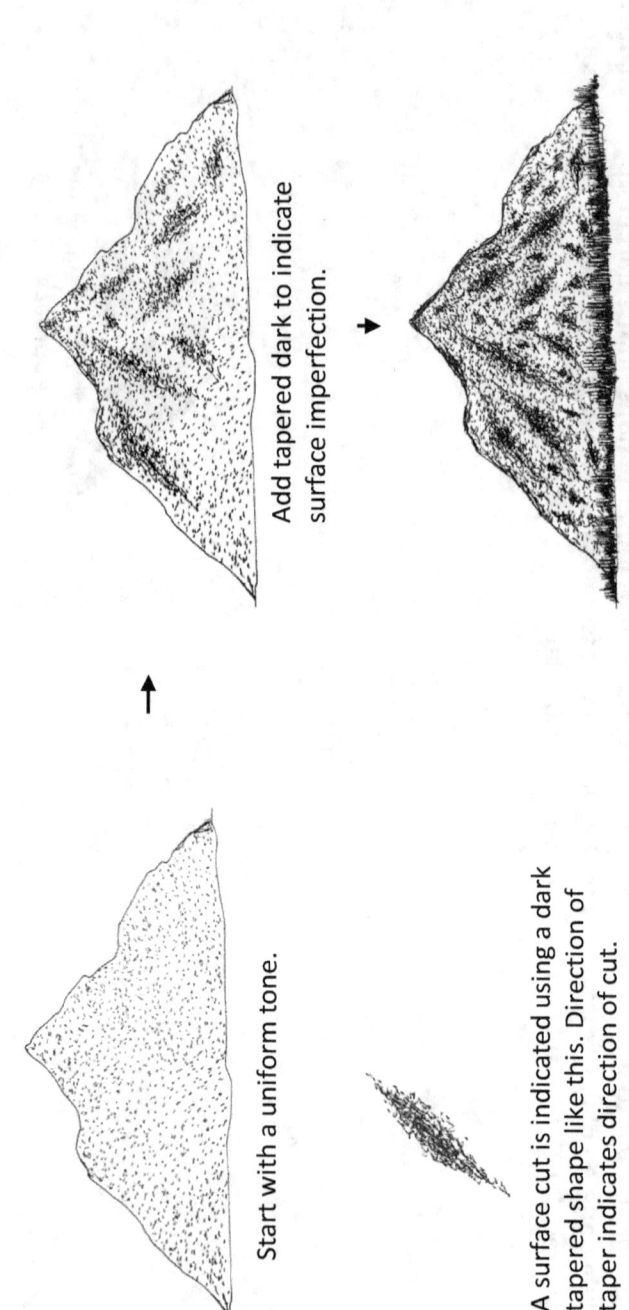

Start with a uniform tone.

A surface cut is indicated using a dark tapered shape like this. Direction of taper indicates direction of cut.

Add tapered dark to indicate surface imperfection.

Adjust the tone and volume of cuts to your liking.

Drawing Mountains with Surface Imperfections, Continued:

Surface imperfections should be added in irregular pleasing manner with different sizes and orientations. For a bigger cut, there should be variation in tone in the cut with center darker and lighter tone towards the edges.

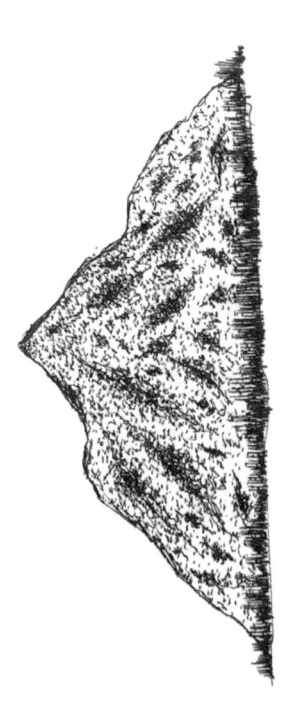

Notice the irregular pleasing distribution of cuts. Use of different sizes and orientation gives it more plausible feel.

Notice the tonal distribution of a bigger cut. Edges are lighter as more light reaches there compared to the center.

Drawing Mountains with Surface Imperfections, Size Matters:

When drawing at a bigger size, more volume of cuts can be indicated as there is more area to work with. For smaller mountain drawings, it is better to use few larger cuts. Adding more volume of cuts at smaller size will result in dark mess.

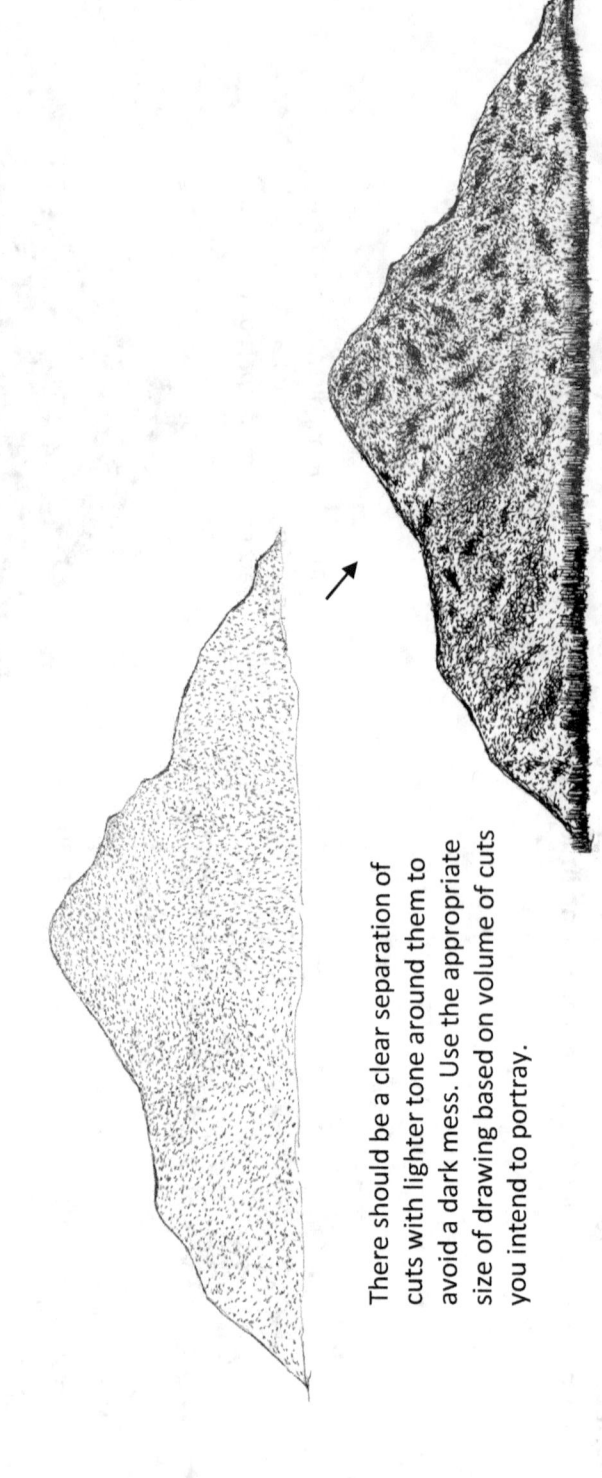

There should be a clear separation of cuts with lighter tone around them to avoid a dark mess. Use the appropriate size of drawing based on volume of cuts you intend to portray.

Activity: Texture Following Mountains by Indicating Cuts:

Texture mountains below by indicating surface irregularities using cuts as discussed earlier.

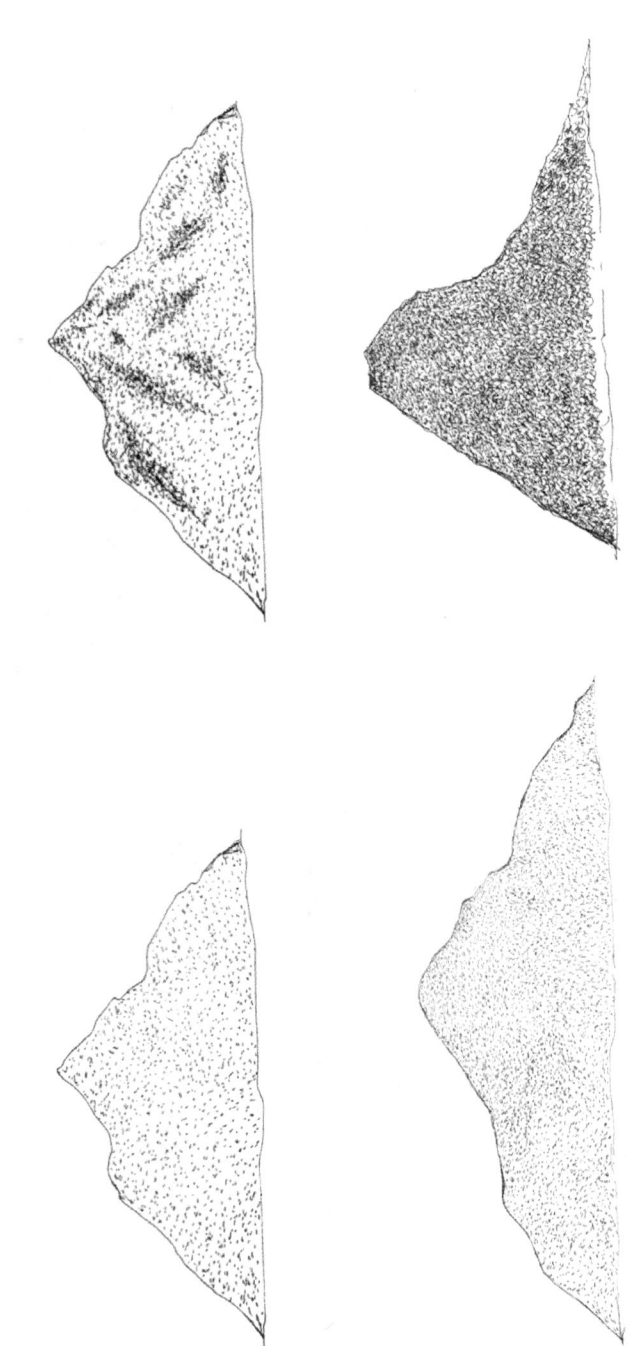

Tonal Distribution Around a Cut:

If there is a sudden tonal change leading to a cut, then it indicates a sudden change in plain of cut where as a gradual tonal change indicates slower curvature change leading to center of cut.

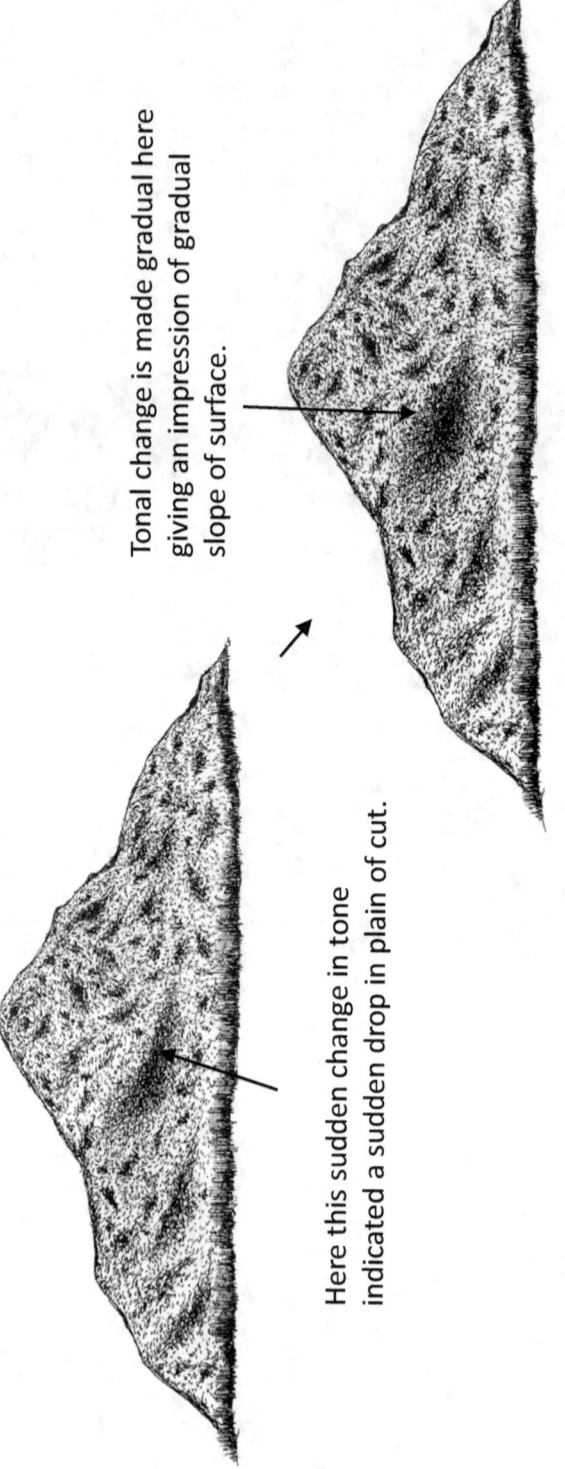

Tonal change is made gradual here giving an impression of gradual slope of surface.

Here this sudden change in tone indicated a sudden drop in plain of cut.

Use combination of sudden and gradual tonal changes for cuts to add interest.

Intensity of Tonal Change:

By now it should be understood that it is tonal change that indicates a change of Plain to our mind. Two plains at different angle to each other will have different volume of light falling on them from the same light source. The intensify of tonal change can be used to create different feel for the mountain as shown below.

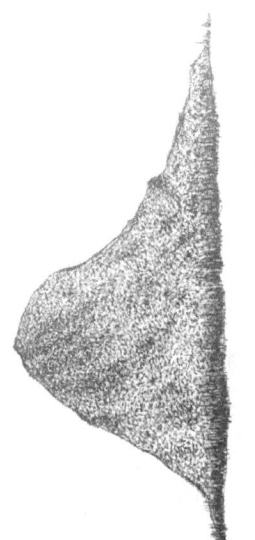

Another example. Play with different levels of tonal change to see the effect you get.

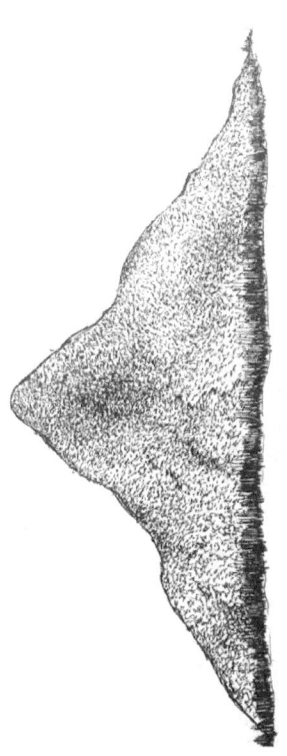

Low intensity of tonal change is used above. Very few dark tones are 'sprinkled' to give more visual interest.

Use intensity of tonal change that is appropriate to bring out the feel you desire.

Drawing Mountains with Surface Imperfections, More Examples:

This is a very flexible approach. By using different shape of mountain outline along with different sizes and volume for cuts, mountains with very different feel can be drawn. Following are some more examples.

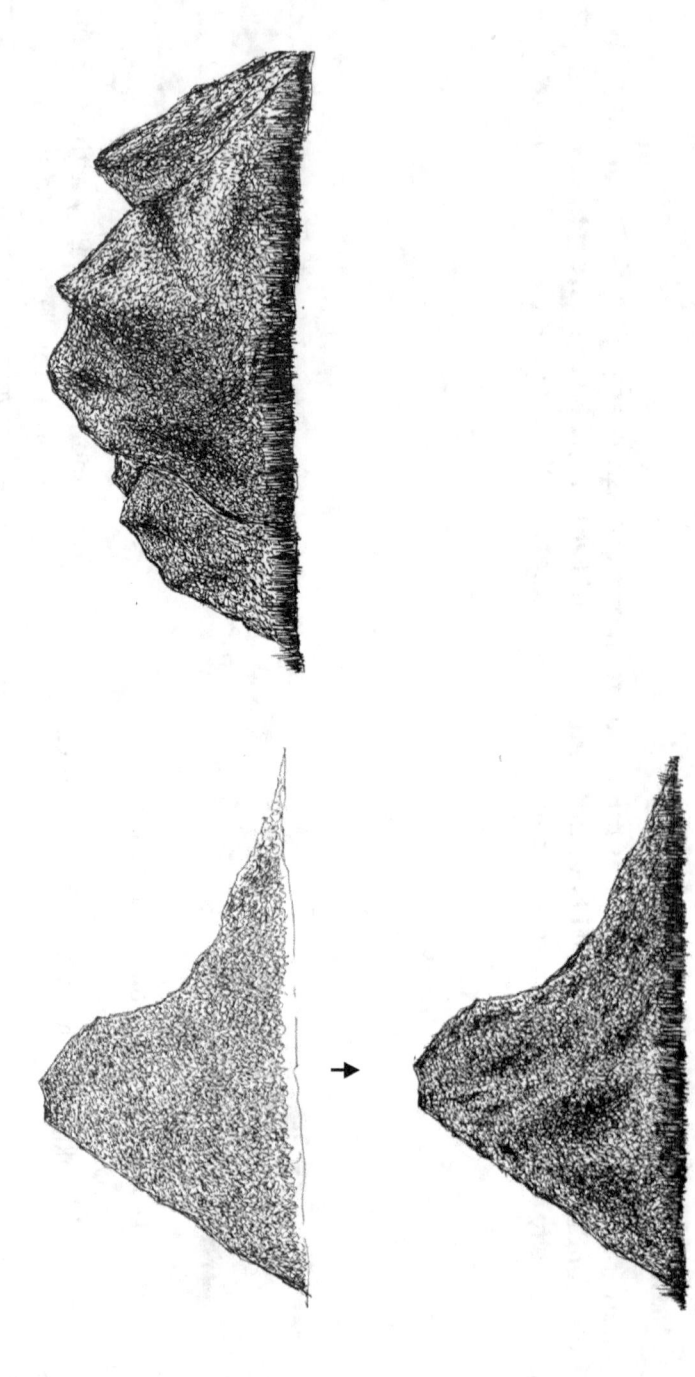

Combining Two Approaches:

Now we combine the 2 approaches to create mountains with angular plains and surface imperfections. Key is to create surface imperfections in the middle part of mountain.

Angular plains are also small and don't extend too deep into the mountain. This gives space to use imperfections there.

In the middle part of mountain, surface imperfections can be used.

Combining Two Approaches , Continued:

Rest of texturing is as we saw before. Note that mountain need to be drawn at relatively bigger size to have space to create imperfections in its middle part.

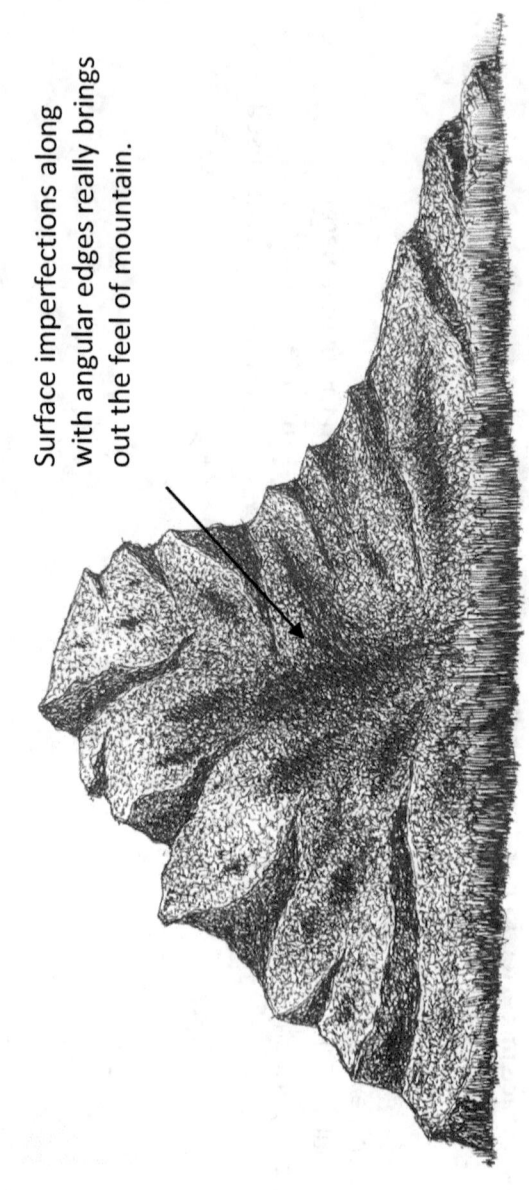

Surface imperfections along with angular edges really brings out the feel of mountain.

Activity: Combining Two Approaches:

Finish the following mountain as discussed earlier by creating angular pians from the edges and surface irregularities in the middle.

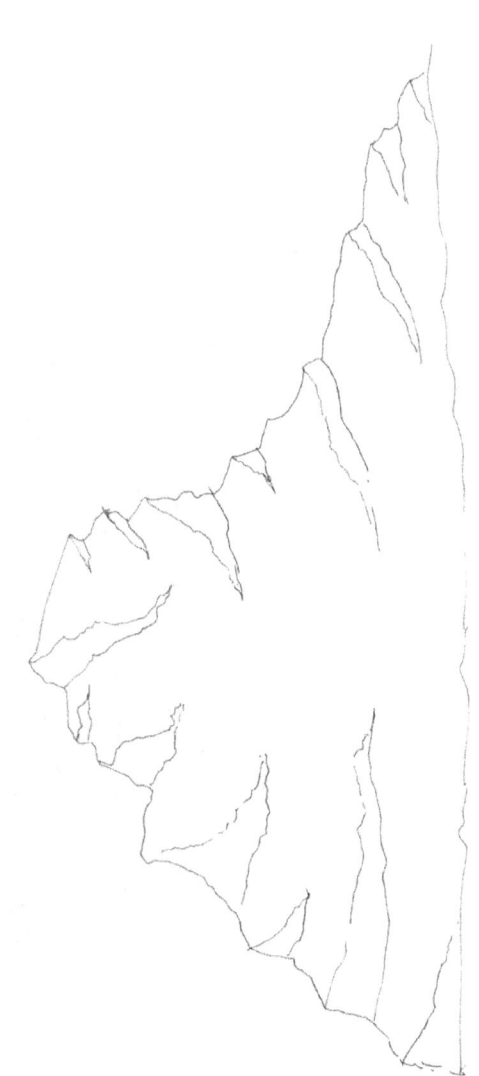

Combining Two Approaches , Another Example:

Following is another example of combining the two approaches. There is no limit to such mountains you can draw from your imagination.

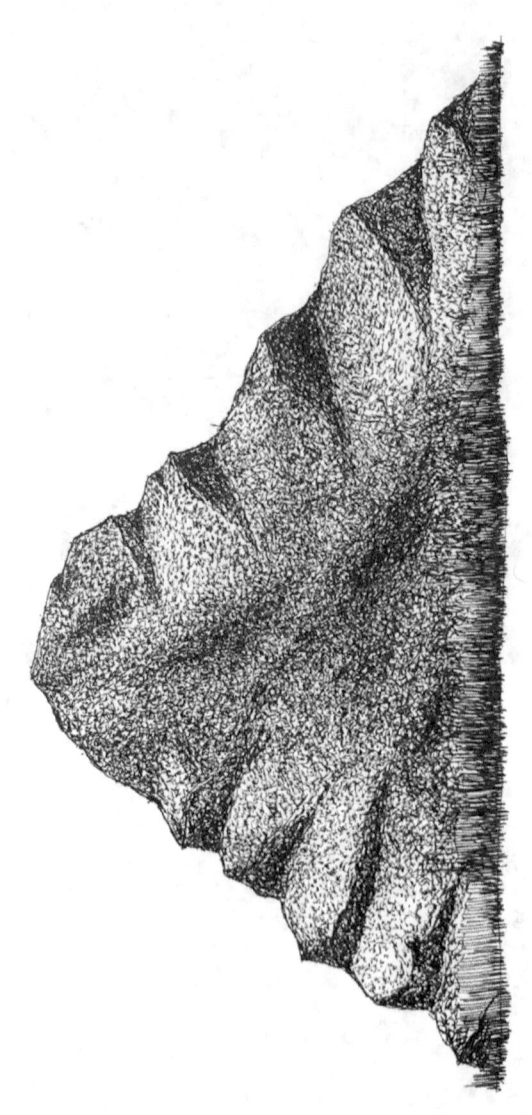

Indicating a Cut with Parallel Lines:

Earlier we saw how to use dots and ticks in a tapered shape to indicate a cut. A cut can be indicated with parallel lines as well. Rest of the process for drawing mountain is similar to what we saw before.

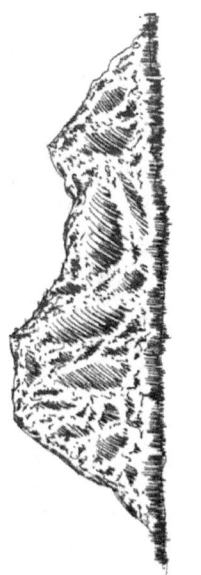

Indicating a Cut with
parallel lines.

Cuts are always
drawn tapered

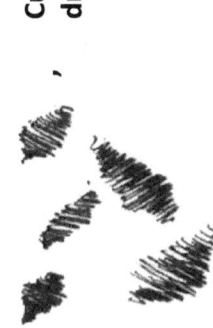

Use tapered shape as discussed
previously. Angle of lines indicates
angle of cut.

Parallel lines are used to indicate
surface irregularities in the
mountain above. Step by step
process is discussed next.

How to Draw a Mountain with Surface Irregularities:

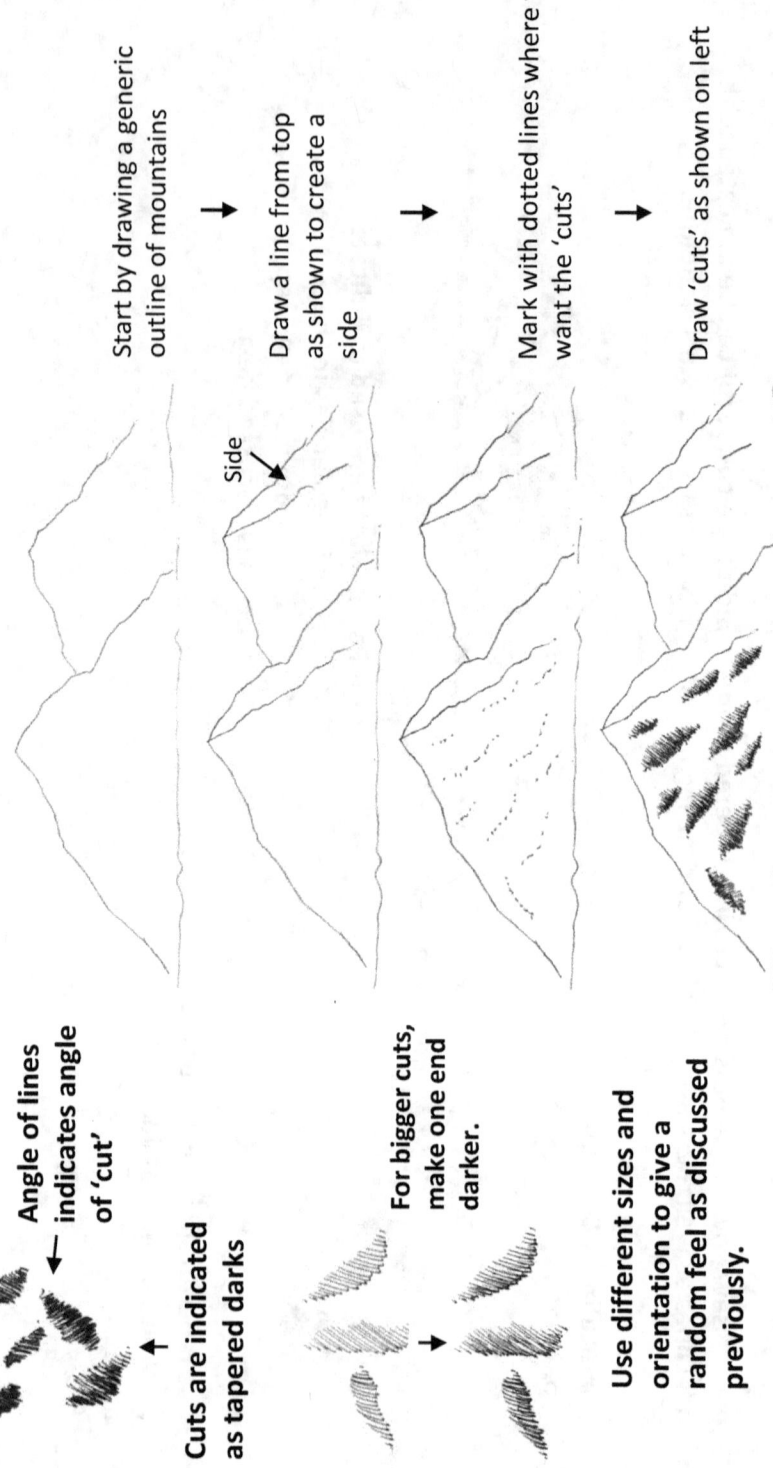

Start by drawing a generic outline of mountains

Draw a line from top as shown to create a side

Side

Mark with dotted lines where you want the 'cuts'

Draw 'cuts' as shown on left

Angle of lines indicates angle of 'cut'

Cuts are indicated as tapered darks

For bigger cuts, make one end darker.

Use different sizes and orientation to give a random feel as discussed previously.

For more information visit www.pendrawings.me/getstarted

How to Draw a Mountain Surface Irregularities, Continued:

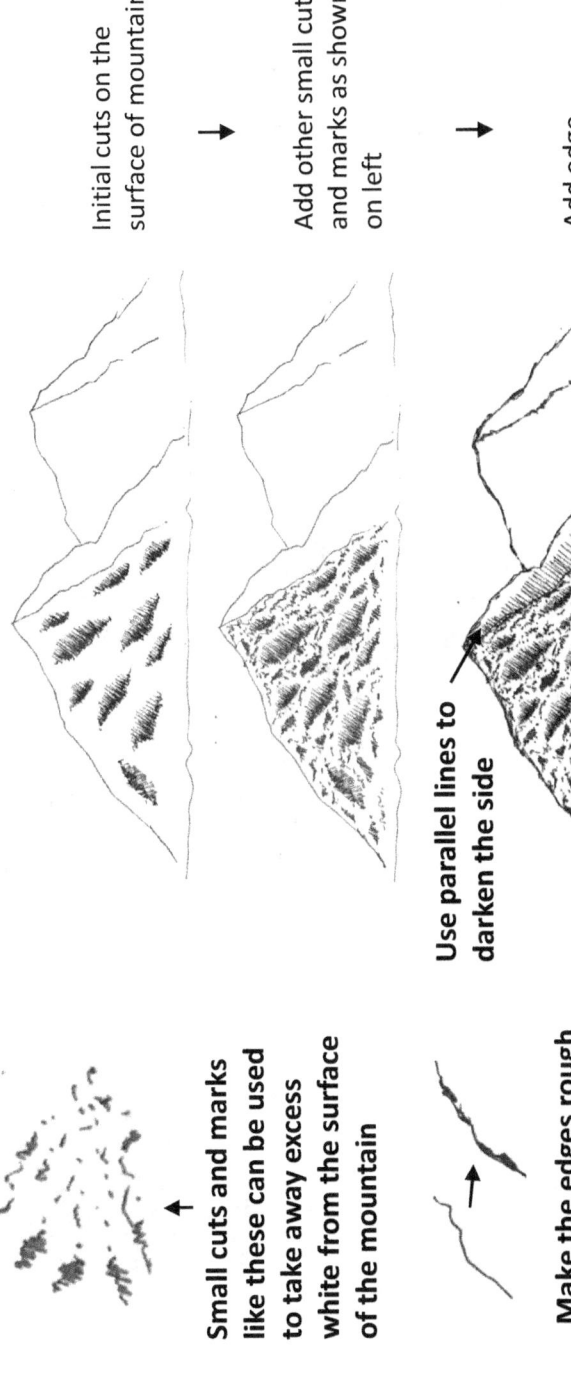

Initial cuts on the surface of mountain

→

Add other small cuts and marks as shown on left

→

Add edge imperfection per instructions on left

Small cuts and marks like these can be used to take away excess white from the surface of the mountain

Use parallel lines to darken the side

Make the edges rough in this manner by darkening the outline

Add a tree line to the base

For more information visit www.pendrawings.me/getstarted

How to Draw a Mountain Surface Irregularities, Continued:

Mountain needs to be given a base tone. Earlier dots and ticks were used for this purpose. In addition to cuts, parallel lines can also be used to provide base tone.

Cuts can be indicated on the side as well

Add 'cuts' to the side

→

Finish the other mountain similarly. Use parallel lines to give additional tone.

→

Finish with grass as ground cover

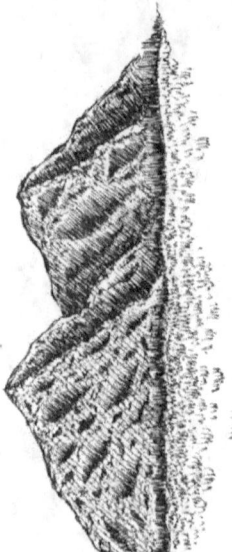

Hatching lines can be used to give a layer of base tone. Other techniques for adding base tone are discussed later.

←

For more information visit www.pendrawings.me/getstarted

Darkening and Shading Mountains:

When drawing a mountain range, darken them in the following manner. Some of this was also discussed earlier when using dots and ticks for texturing.

Base of slice is darkest

Direction of Sun.

Darken the base of slice the most. Leave the top slightly lighter. This creates the distinction between the front and back mountain

In a mountain range, this part of mountain behind receives less light and should be darkened with a set of hatching lines

Technically, there should be tonal variation across this surface of mountain as well, but usually it is not necessary. Making the slice darker is enough to convey the right feel

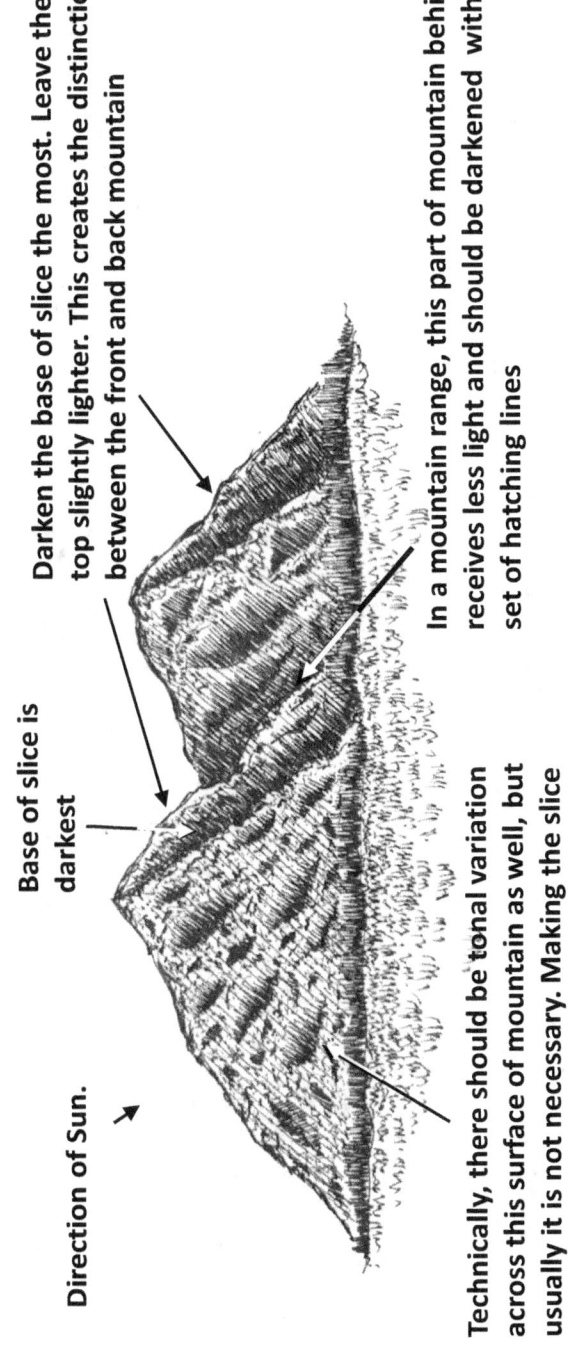

For more information visit www.pendrawings.me/getstarted

Adding Base Tone to the Mountain:

A Mountain generally has a darker base tone. The white of paper needs to be taken away to give a darker base tone. This can be done in following manner.

Using dots and ticks for base Tone:

Using wiggly lines for base tone:

Using Hatching lines

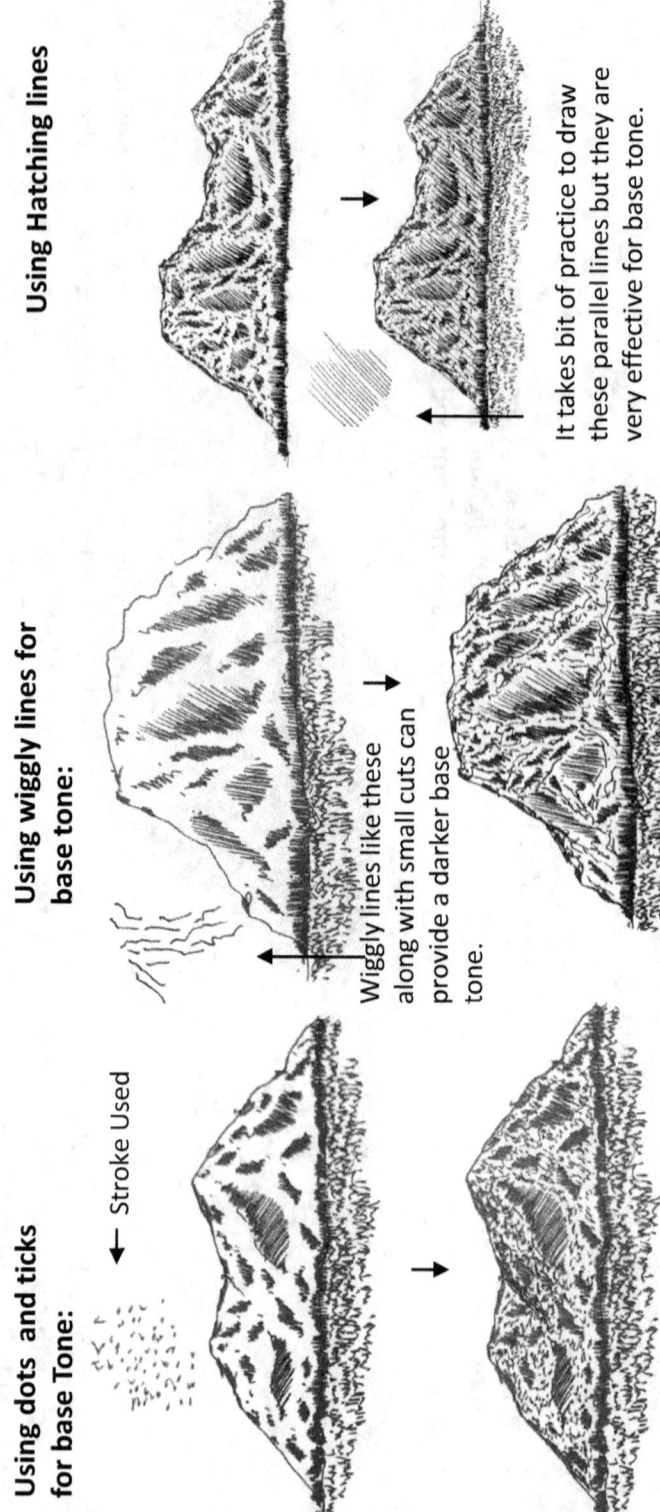

Stroke Used

Wiggly lines like these along with small cuts can provide a darker base tone.

It takes bit of practice to draw these parallel lines but they are very effective for base tone.

As you can see above, a darker base tone gives a nice feeling to the mountain. Level of base tone is a matter of personal preference.

For more information visit www.pendrawings.me/getstarted

Level of Base Tone:

More base tone can be used to give an overall darker feel to the mountain. Experiment with different levels to see what you prefer.

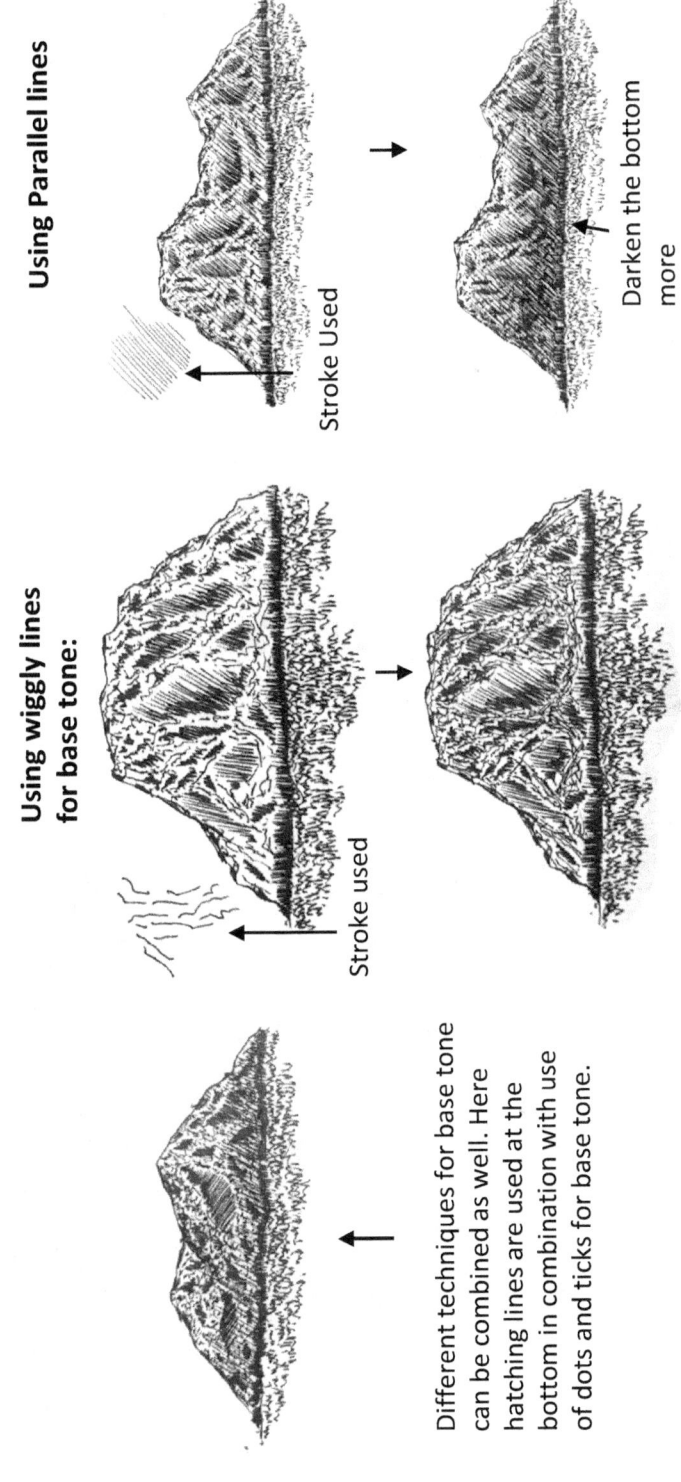

Using Parallel lines

Stroke Used

Darken the bottom more

Using wiggly lines for base tone:

Stroke used

Different techniques for base tone can be combined as well. Here hatching lines are used at the bottom in combination with use of dots and ticks for base tone.

Direction of Shading the Slice:

The angle of hatching lines used to shade the slice gives different feel. Experiment with both.

This direction of hatching lines gives feel of flat appearance for the slice

This direction of hatching lines gives impression of deep groove in the slice. This is mostly used in the examples in this book.

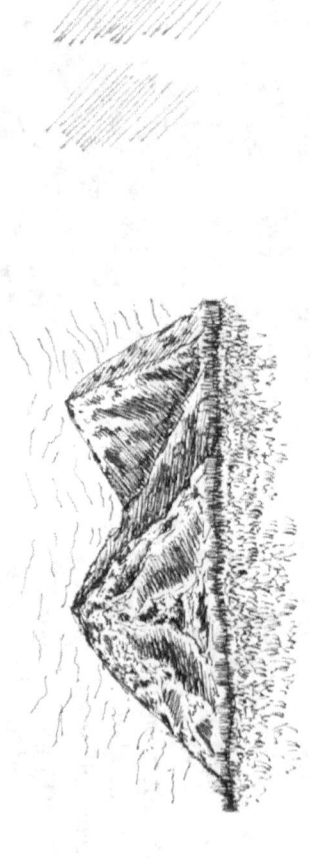

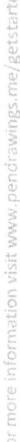

For more information visit www.pendrawings.me/getstarted

Additional Examples of Mountains with Surface Irregularities:

Following are some additional examples of using this technique. As you can see below, by changing the shape, size and location of these cuts and by using different techniques for base tone, different feel for mountains can be obtained.

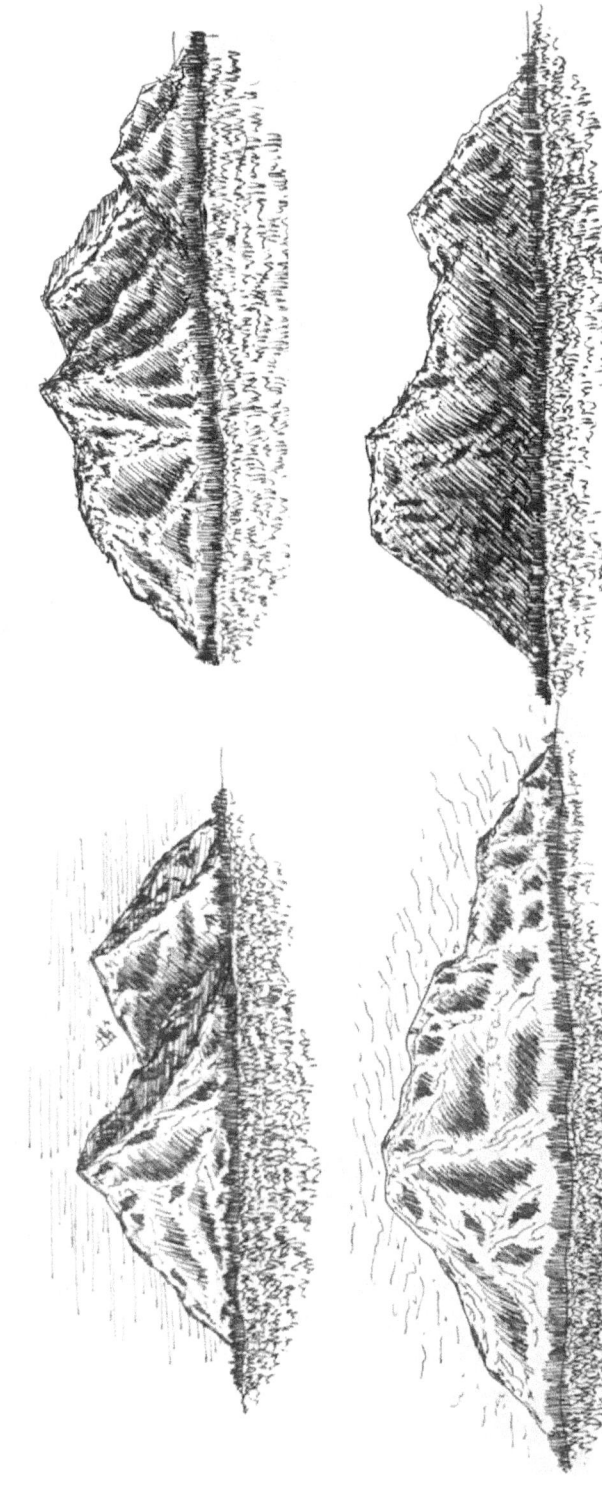

Sky/Clouds provides a nice backdrop to mountains. They are covered in detail in another volume. Pl. visit www.pendrawings.me/workbooks for more information.

Comparing Dots/Ticks with Parallel Lines:

In the beginning we looked at dots and ticks as the stroke to texture mountain. In last few pages, we used parallel lines (along with other strokes for base tone) to indicate cuts. As you can see below, even though technique is the same, stroke used and its manner of usage has a big impact on final outcome. Experiment with different strokes to develop your repertoire.

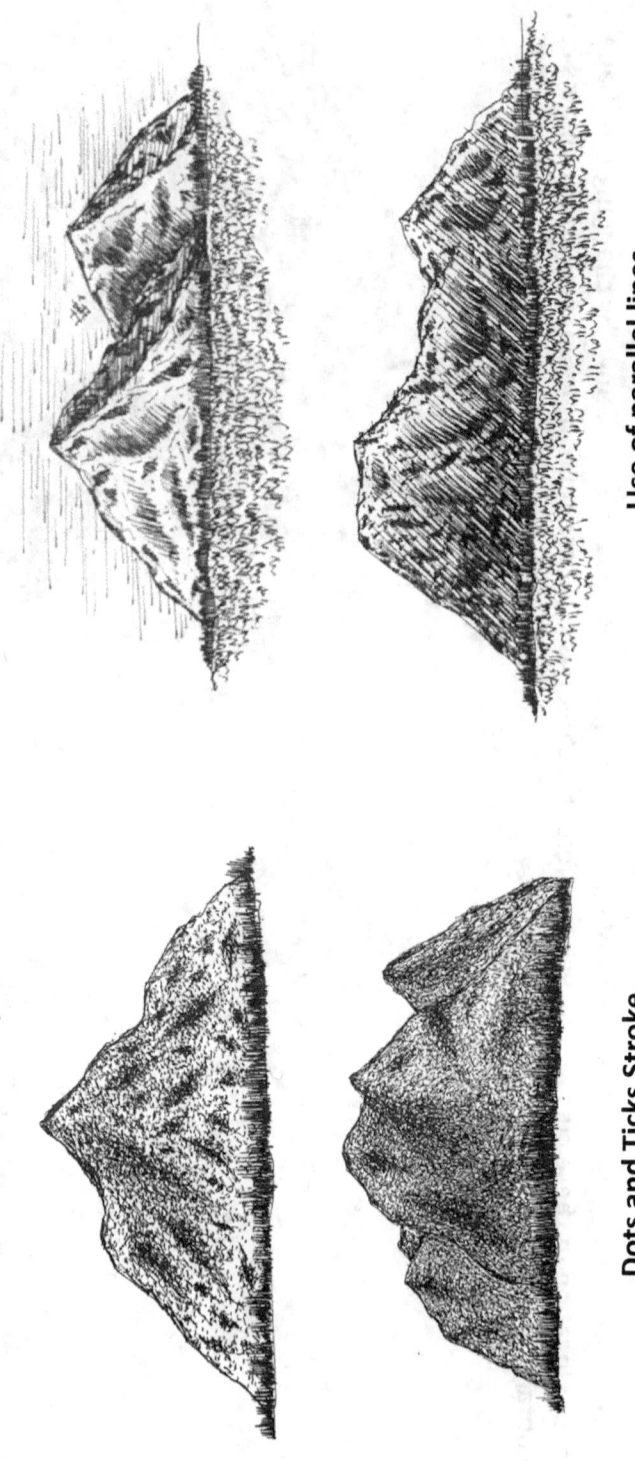

Dots and Ticks Stroke.

Use of parallel lines.

For more information visit www.pendrawings.me/getstarted

Activity Drawing Mountains:

Practice drawing mountains in the following outlines per earlier instructions. Use parallel lines for cuts along with different techniques for base tone.

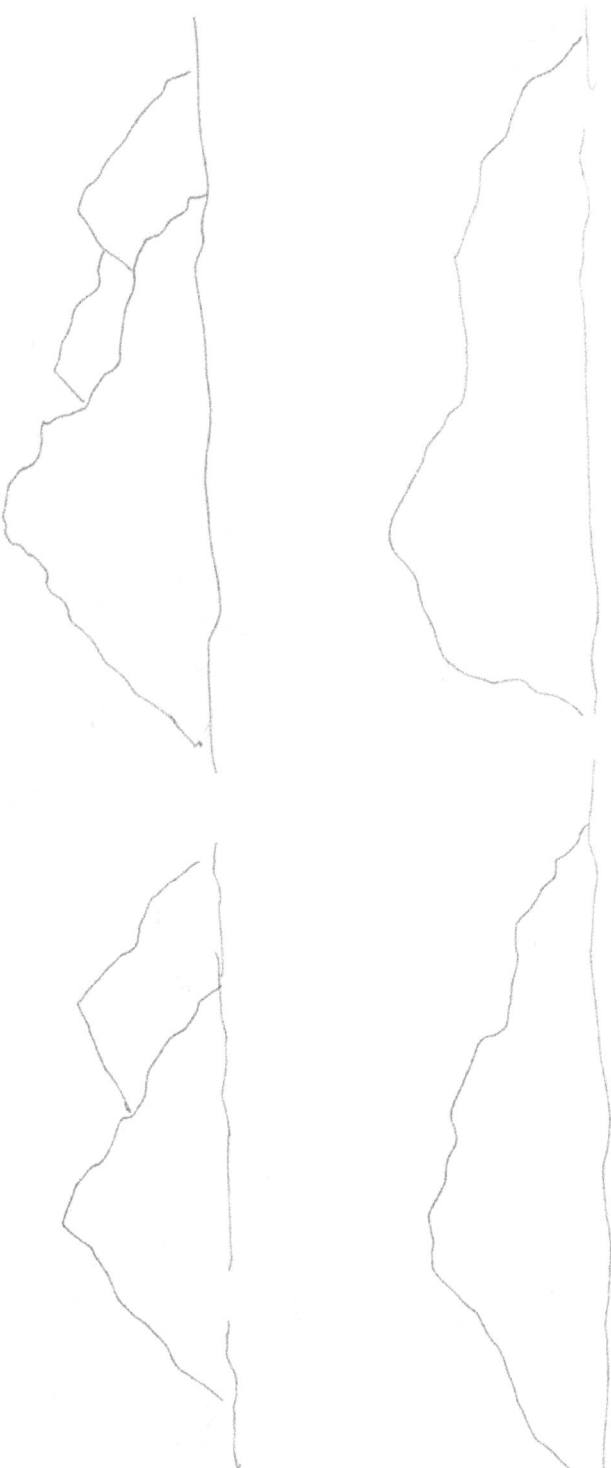

For more information visit www.pendrawings.me/getstarted

Indicating Surface Imperfections with Projections:

Another way to indicate surface imperfection is through use of 'Projection'. They indicate a protrusion from the surface. This brings out roughness and feel of mountain. They are draw as shown below.

How to draw a Projection:

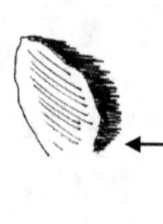

Start by drawing a shape like the one on the left

Draw parallel lines from the sides to define depth

Use lines on the top to define surface curvature

Group of Projections:

Draw the outline of behind projection from the edge of projection in front

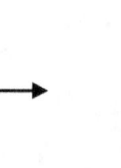

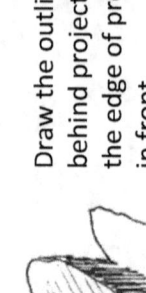

Draw parallel lines from the sides to define depth

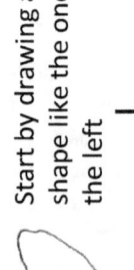

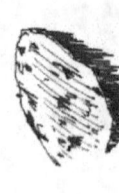

To blend projection with surrounding surface, taper the height as shown

Edge irregularities and tapered crevices can be added as well

For more information visit www.pendrawings.me/getstarted

Activity Drawing Projections:

Practice drawing Projections in the following outlines per earlier instructions. Draw some of your own.

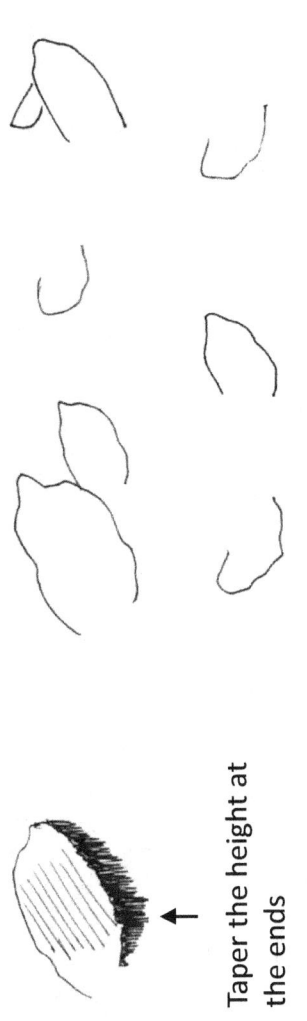

Taper the height at
the ends

For more information visit www.pendrawings.me/getstarted

How to Draw a Mountain with Projections:

In this technique, 'Projections' are made on the surface of the mountains.

Use different shape, sizes and orientation for projections to make it interesting.

Use bigger projections in the center and smaller towards the edges

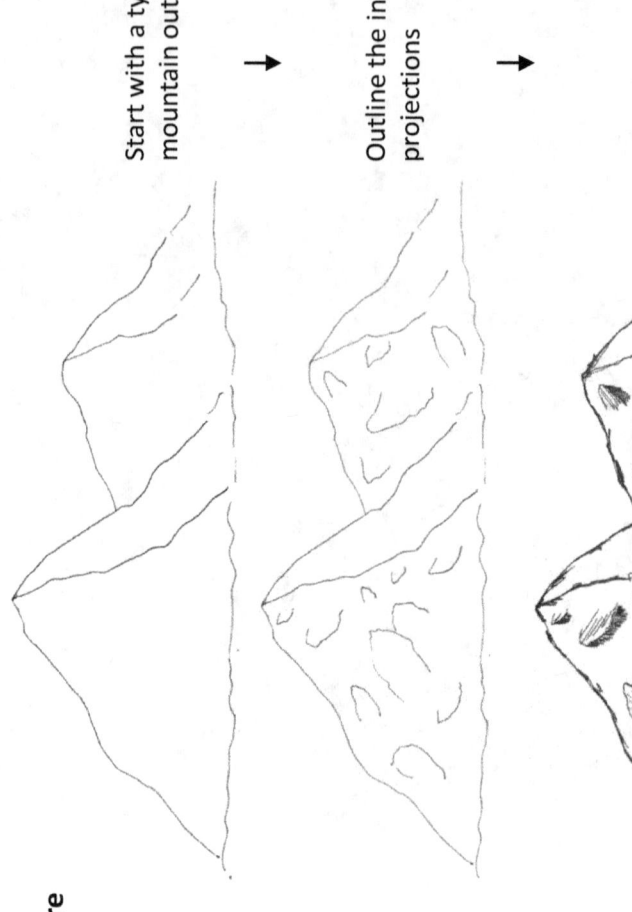

Start with a typical mountain outline

→

Outline the initial projections

→

Draw the initial projections

For more information visit www.pendrawings.me/getstarted

How to Draw a Mountain with Projections, Continued:

Projections can be combined with cuts we saw earlier to create surface imperfections.

Different techniques to add base tone is discussed earlier.

Add small projections and cuts to cover the surface

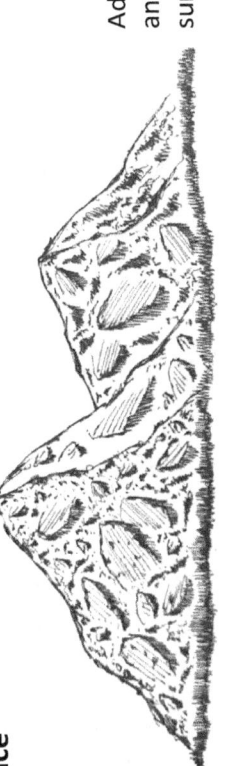

→

Darken the slice and base of back mountains to bring out contrast and depth

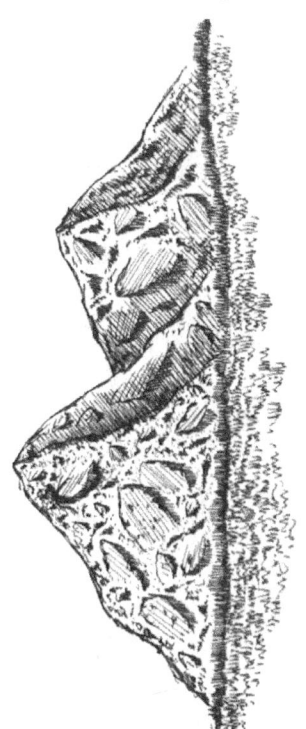

For more information visit www.pendrawings.me/getstarted

Some More Examples of Projections:

By using different sizes, shapes and orientation for these projections, different mountains can be easily drawn from your imagination.

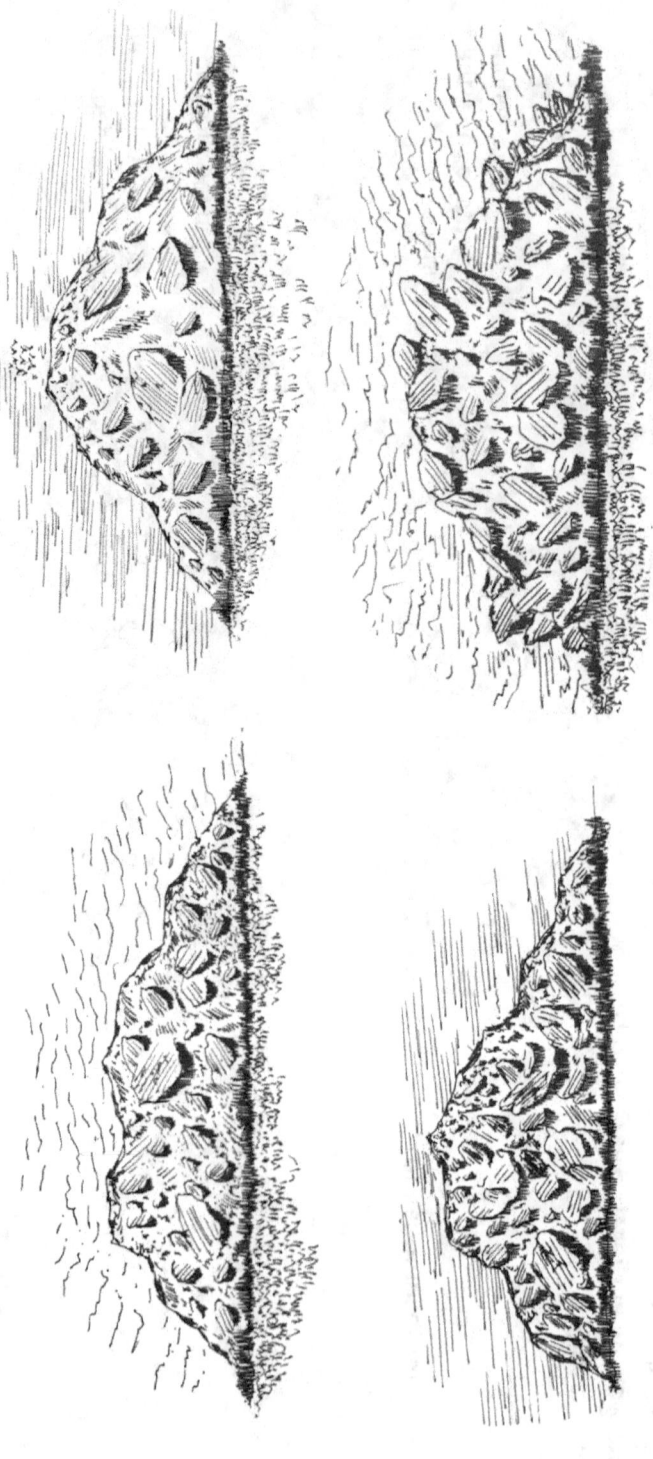

Here projections are used for edges as well.

For more information visit www.pendrawings.me/getstarted

Activity: Drawing Mountains with Projections:

Add Projections and finish texturing of following outlines per earlier instructions.

Use of Surface Contours:

It is very important to understand that there should be no loss in our perception and understanding of surface contour of a mountain. If this is the case then the drawing looks incomplete.

In this area more surface irregularities can be added to create 'implicit' surface definition or contour lines can be used to define the surface form.

In this significant area there is no indication of surface definition without which the drawing looks incomplete.

For more information visit www.pendrawings.me/getstarted

Use of Surface Contours:

Surface contour is indicated by use of parallel lines where the direction of parallel lines indicate the surface form. Adding contour lines bring out the form of inside of the mountain.

Notice the use of contour lines in different directions to give angular form to inside of the mountain.

Such contour lines indicate the surface form and together gives a form to the mountain.

Not all white of the inside of mountain needs to be covered with contour lines. There is still some white in the drawing above. Key is to make sure the area of white without surface definition is small enough to not create visual discontinuity. Our mind then implicitly assigns contour to the white space based on surrounding contour definition. This also helps to keep the drawing clean.

For more information visit www.pendrawing-.me/getstarted

Surface Contours vs Surface Cuts:

Fundamentally, surface contour and cuts do the same primary task of indicating underlying surface form using parallel lines where the orientation of parallel lines indicate the underlying orientation of surface. The difference between the two is in the tonal intensity.

Cut

Contour
Lines

More tone is used in a cut to seek attention and to reinforce surface roughness.

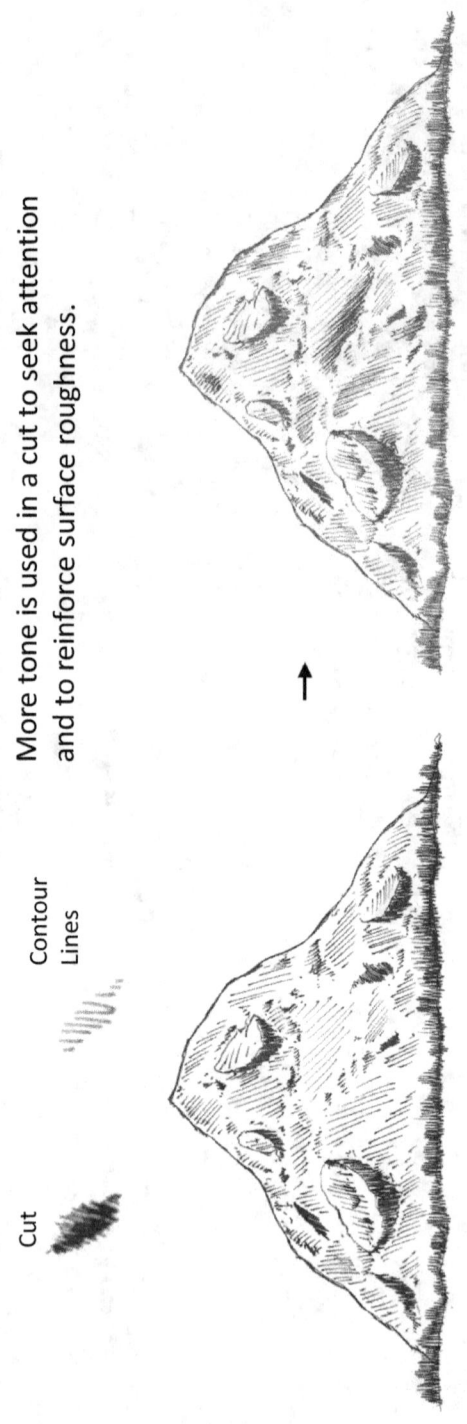

Technically, the tone of different contour surfaces should be in accordance with the amount of light they would receive from an assumed light source as we discussed in detail earlier. But in a small size drawing, it is usually difficult to do. In this case, it is sufficient to indicate more tone for vertically oriented surfaces and less for horizontal contours (this assumes light source overhead).

For more information visit www.pendrawings.me/getstarted

Drawing Mountains with Surface Contours:

A mountain can be drawn just by using surface contours as shown below. In this case mountain is not 'attention seeking' and might be appropriate when this is desired.

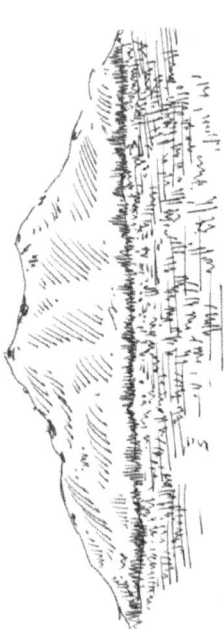

Such 'contour lines' give indication of surface contour. Orientation of lines give orientation of surface contour

Mountains can be drawn using contour lines alone as this example shows. No darker tone makes this mountain bit boring and stay in the background.

By 'sprinkling' some darker tone of a cut makes the mountain more interesting with varied tones.

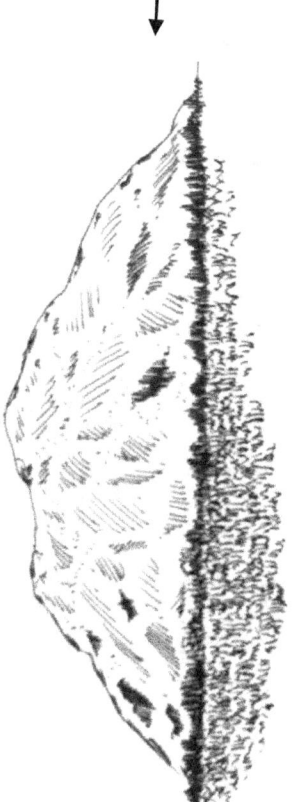

For more information visit www.pendrawings.me/getstarted

Implicit Surface Contours:

It should be understood that some indication of surface form always need to be given. When using dots and ticks, parallel contour lines are not used but instead the tonal variation of dots and ticks gives indication of surface form.

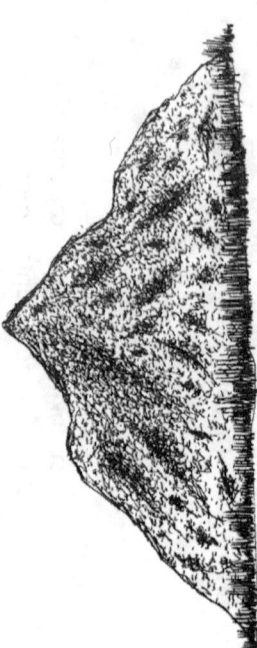

When using dots and ticks for texturing, their tonal variation on the surface implicitly defines surface contour of the mountain.

Contour lines are only used when texturing with parallel lines.

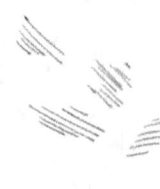

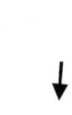

Using high volume of surface imperfections leaves little white. In this case there is no need to use contour lines as our mind doesn't perceive discontinuity of surface definition.

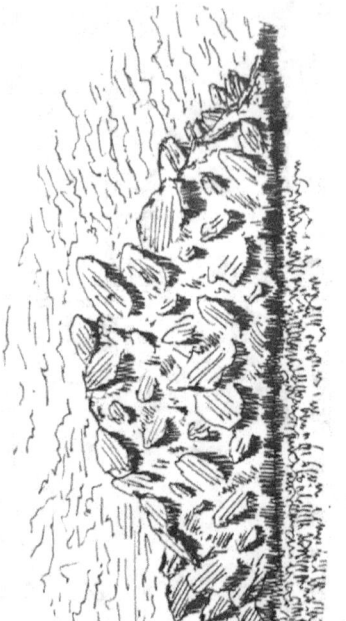

For more information visit www.pendrawings.me/getstarted

Activity Drawing Contour Lines:

Practice drawing contour lines per earlier instructions and as shown below. Try different angles and sizes. You can turn the paper to draw in different directions as well.

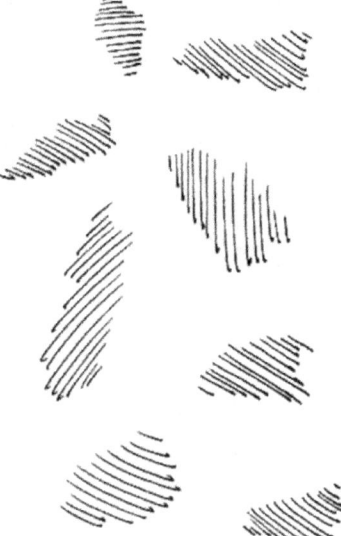

Drawing Projections with Dots and Ticks:

Dots and ticks can also be used to create projections. With just small tapered dark areas, indication of a projection can be given as seen in the drawing below.

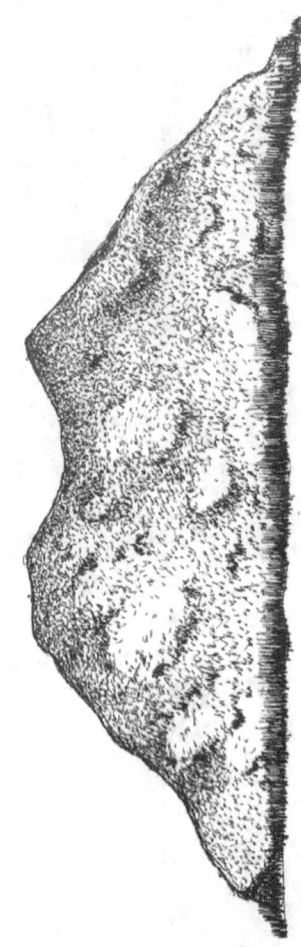

Projections can be indicated using dots and ticks to indicate surface roughness and feel of mountain.

'Designing' the Mountain:

As discussed so far, there are following 3 elements that go into texturing a mountain. You decide on relative use of each in filling the mountain outline and this gives different feel to the mountain.

1. **Main Imperfection:** Start by drawing the main imperfection (cut, projections).
2. **Surface Contours:** In the remaining white, surface contour lines can be added.
3. **Base Tone:** In the end, base tone strokes can be used to further add tone if need be.

Intensity of use of above elements determines the overall feel of your mountain.

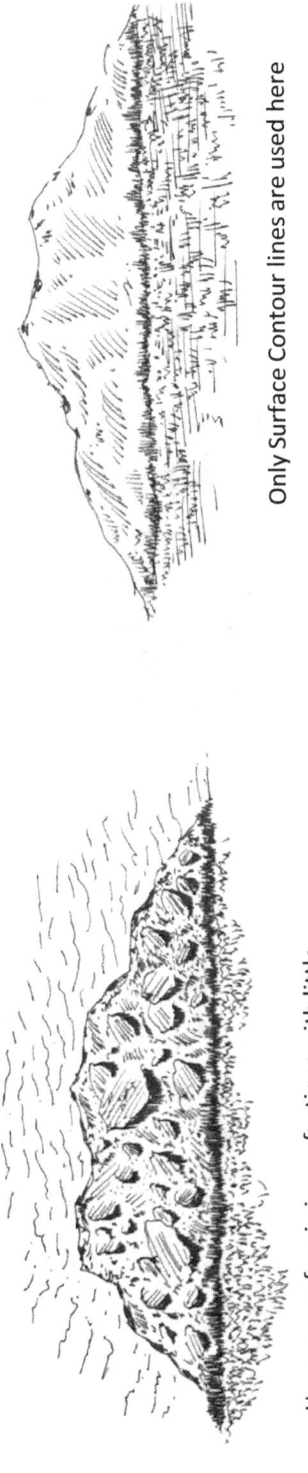

Only Surface Contour lines are used here

Heavy use of main imperfections with little use of surface contours and base tone

Play with different combination of above elements to get different feel in your mountains.

'Designing' the Mountain, Continued:

Here are some more examples. Study them closely to understand how use of different elements affect the feel of the mountain.

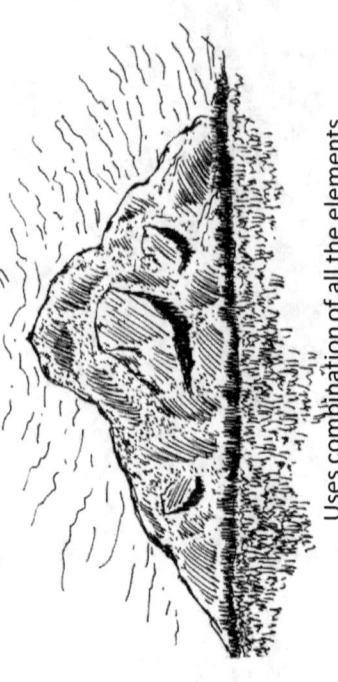

Uses combination of all the elements

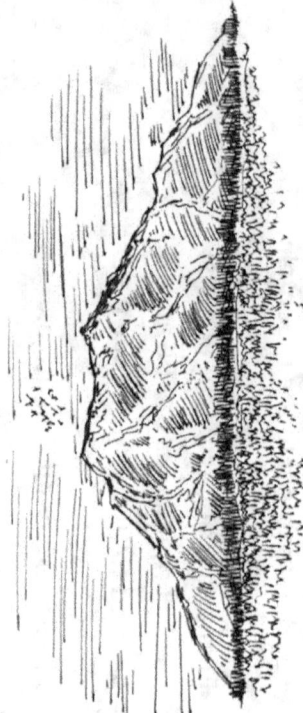

Here contour lines with wiggle lines for base tone is used

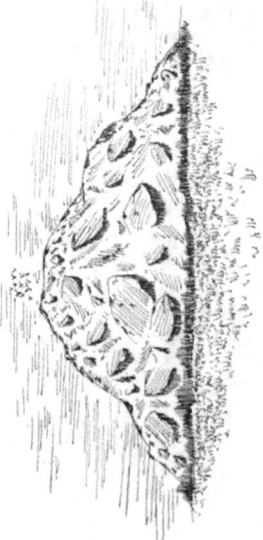

Combination of Main Imperfections along with surface contours

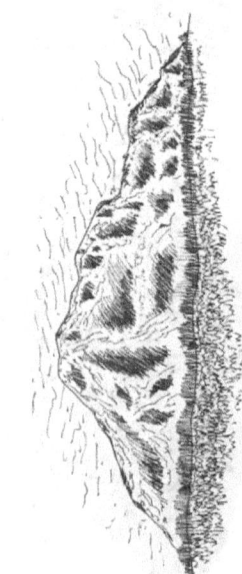

Mainly cuts with use of base tone. Orientation and size of main cuts defines an 'implicit' contour of mountain surface

Activity Drawing Mountains:

Practice drawing mountains in the following outlines per earlier instructions.

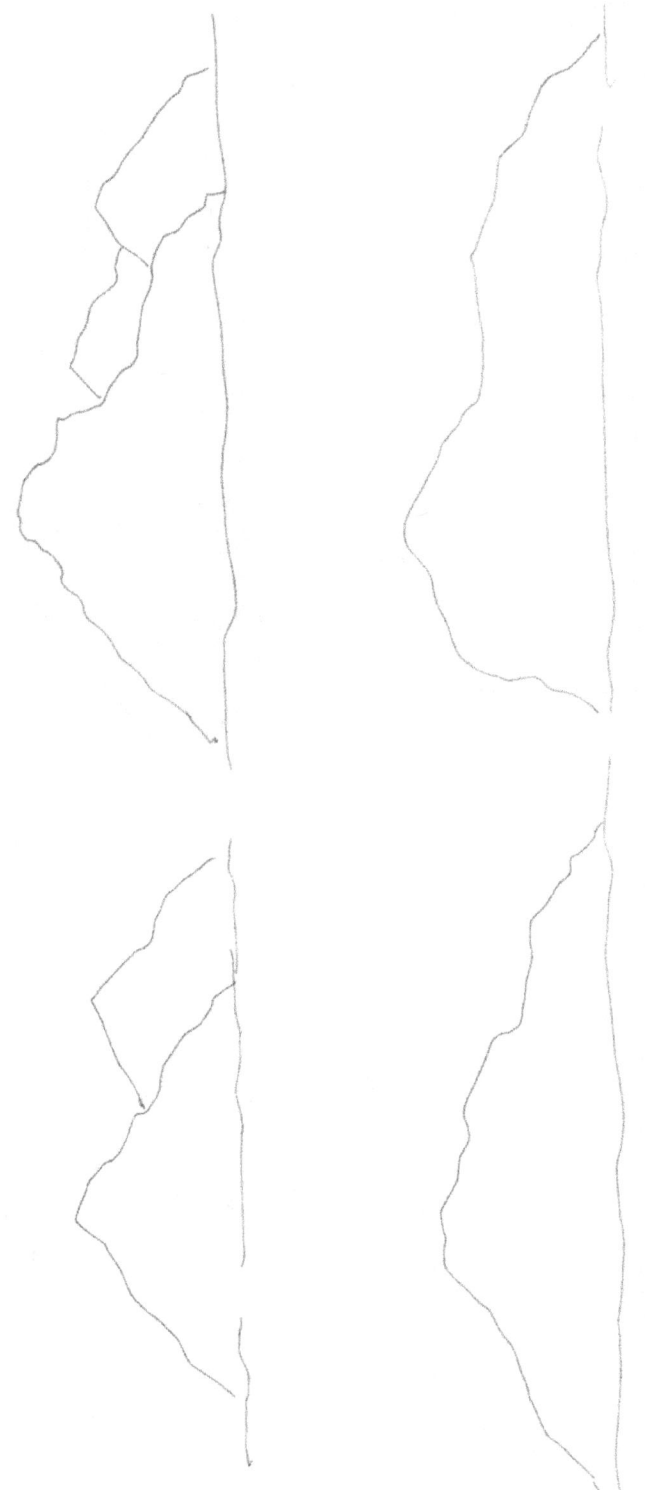

For more information visit www.pendrawings.me/getstarted

Vertical Cuts:

'vertical cuts' can be thought of as a special case of cuts when the direction of cut is vertical. They go very well with projections and can be used together to create mountains very effectively.

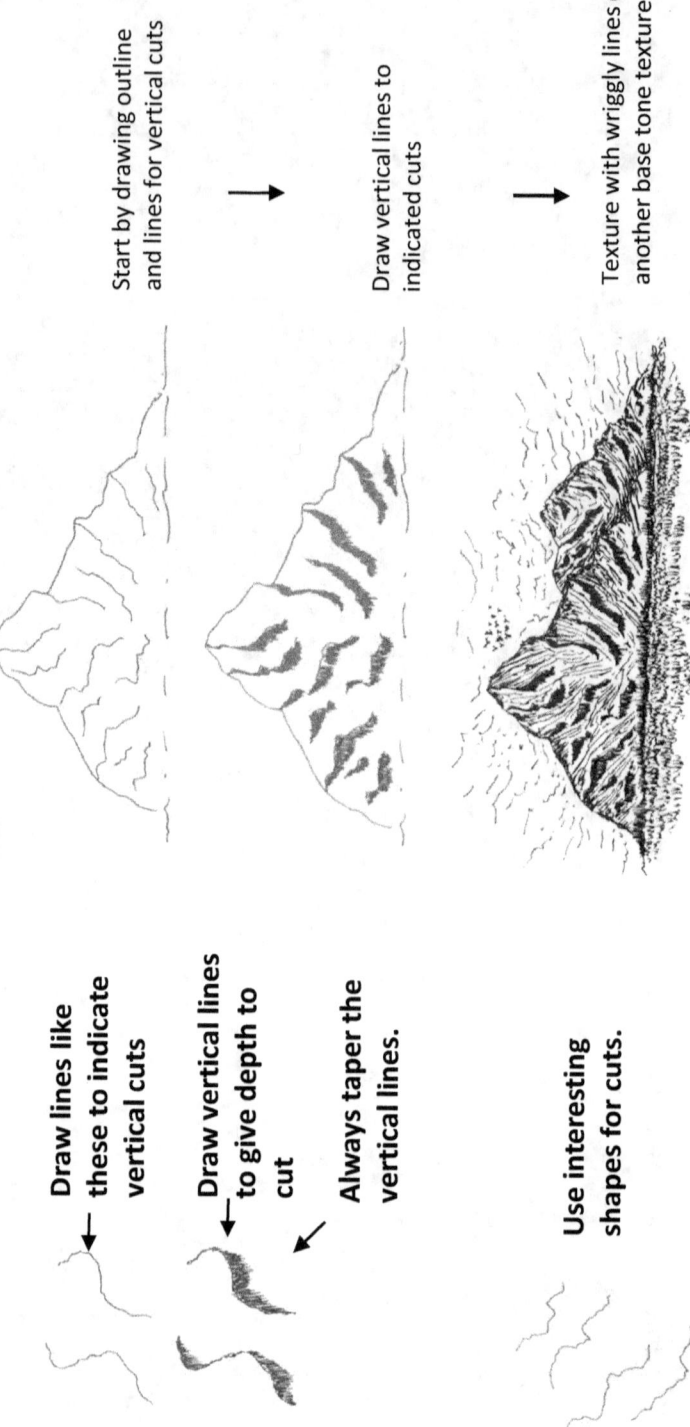

Start by drawing outline and lines for vertical cuts

Draw vertical lines to indicated cuts

Texture with wriggly lines or another base tone texture

Draw lines like these to indicate vertical cuts

Draw vertical lines to give depth to cut

Always taper the vertical lines.

Use interesting shapes for cuts.

Vertical Cuts, Continued:

Here are some more examples of using vertical cuts. Notice the subtle difference in drawing a projection vs a vertical cut but the big difference it has on the visual appearance.

Projection vs Vertical Cut

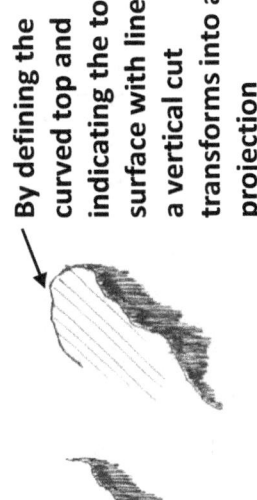

By defining the curved top and indicating the top surface with lines, a vertical cut transforms into a projection

Vertical Cut   Projection

Attempt mountains with mix of projections and vertical cuts. My aim here is to give you different techniques to experiment with and enjoy drawing.

Vertical cuts and projections go very well together to indicate surface imperfections. Here are some more examples:

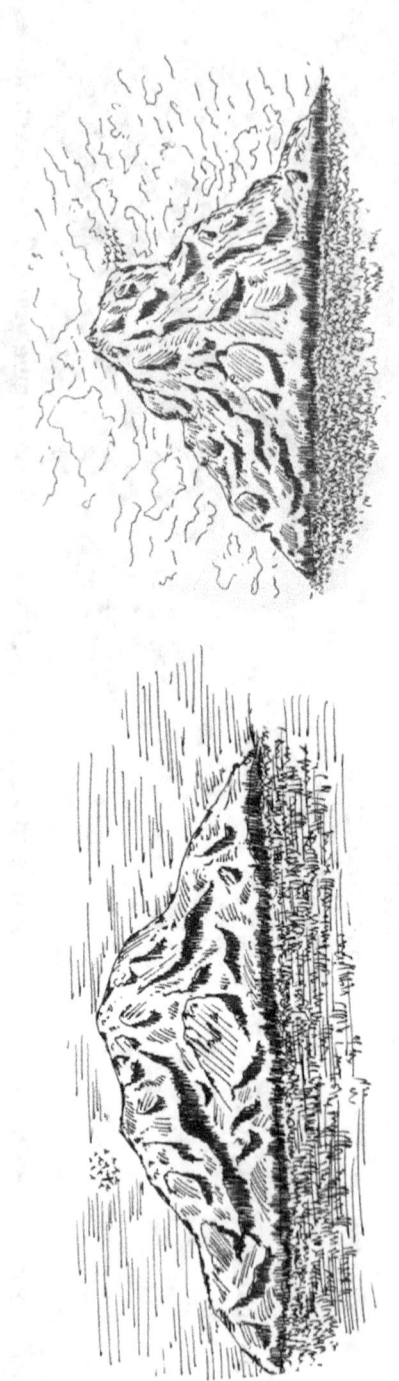

In these examples, projections and vertical cuts are used along with contour lines to create mountains.

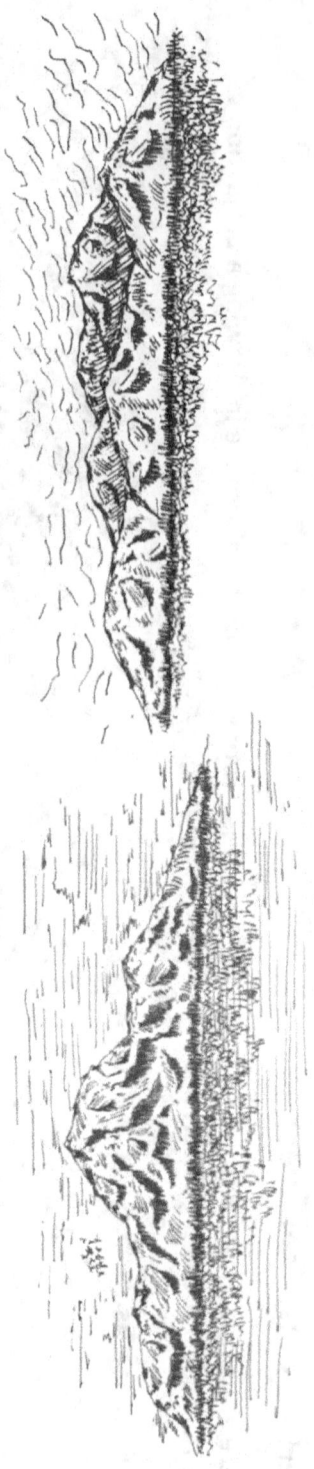

Activity Drawing Mountains:

These are same outlines as before. Try finishing them with combination of projections and vertical cuts.

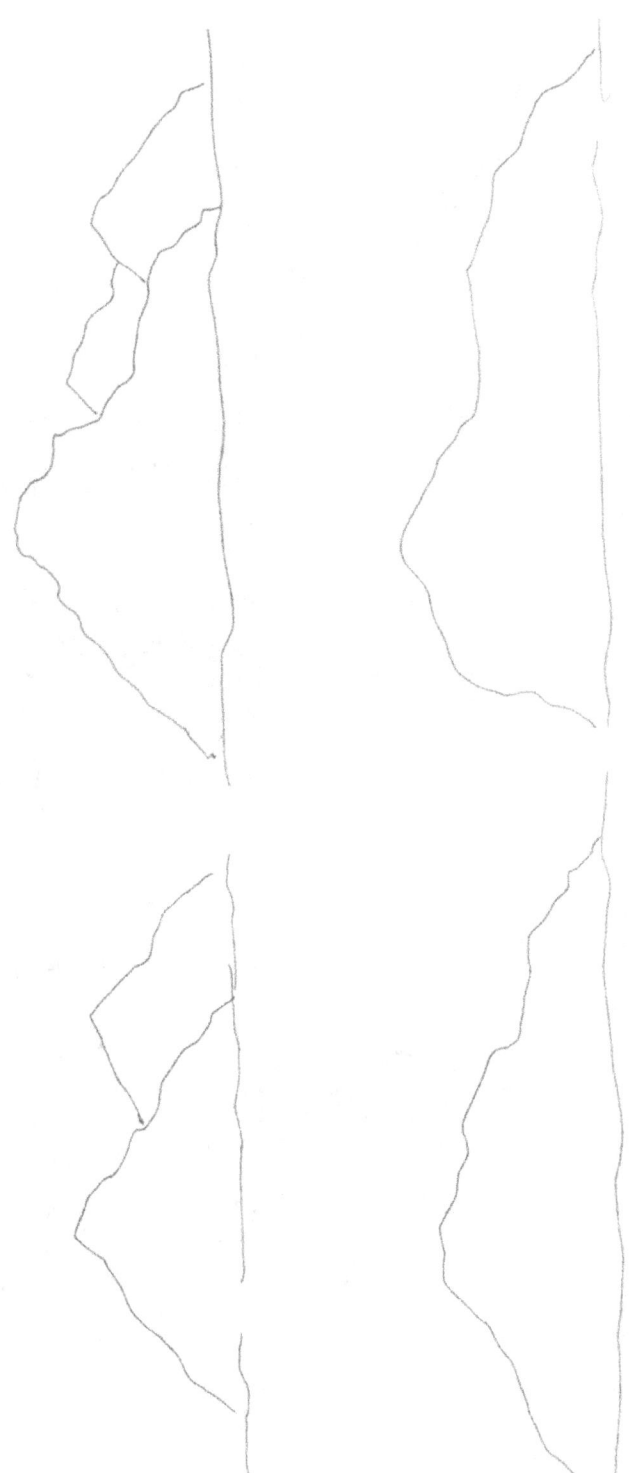

Drawing Stones and Rocks:

Same techniques can also be used to draw stones and rocks as shown below. Just draw them at smaller scale in proportion to other elements as shown below. Drawing stones and other foreground elements like posts, trunks is covered in detail in other workbooks (www.pendrawings.me/workbooks).

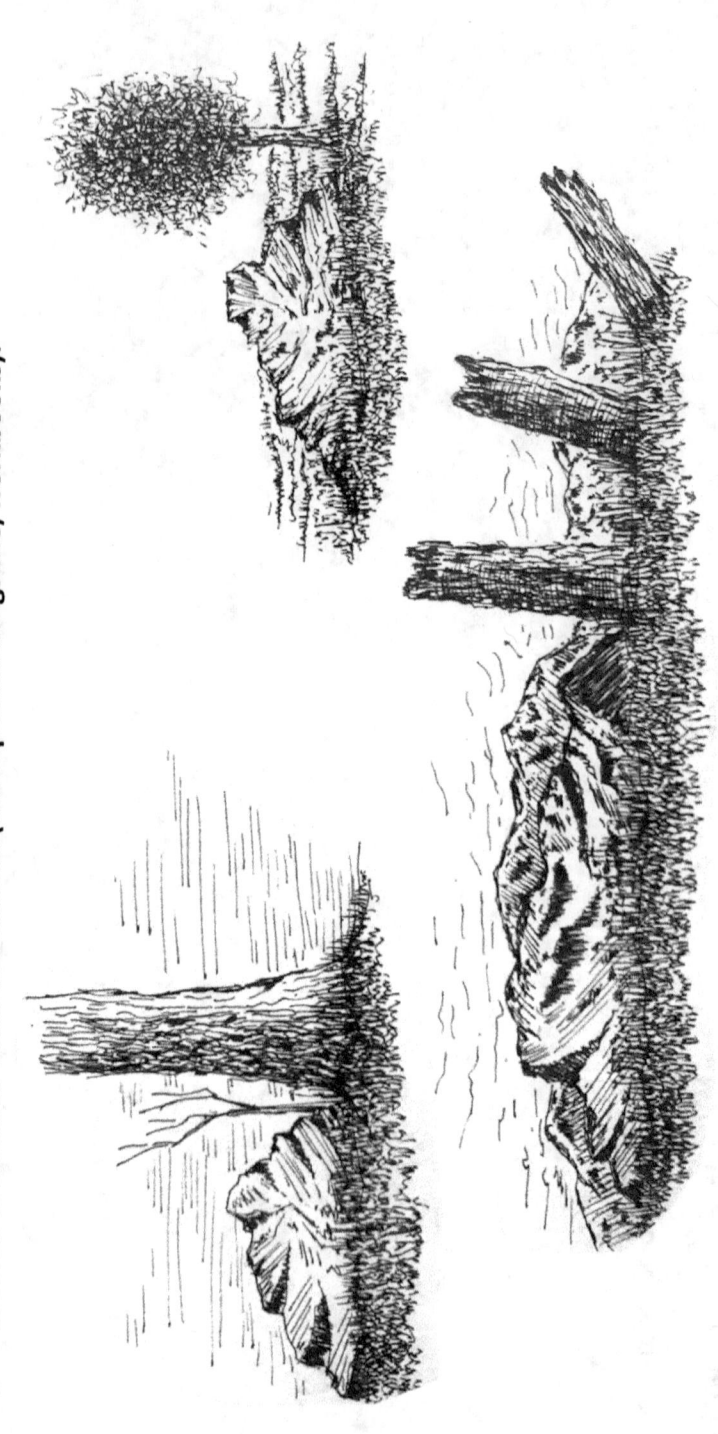

For more information visit www.pendrawings.me/getstarted

Combining Different Techniques:

Different techniques discussed previously can be combined to create mountains with varied feel. Following are 2 such examples. Experiment with combination of different techniques.

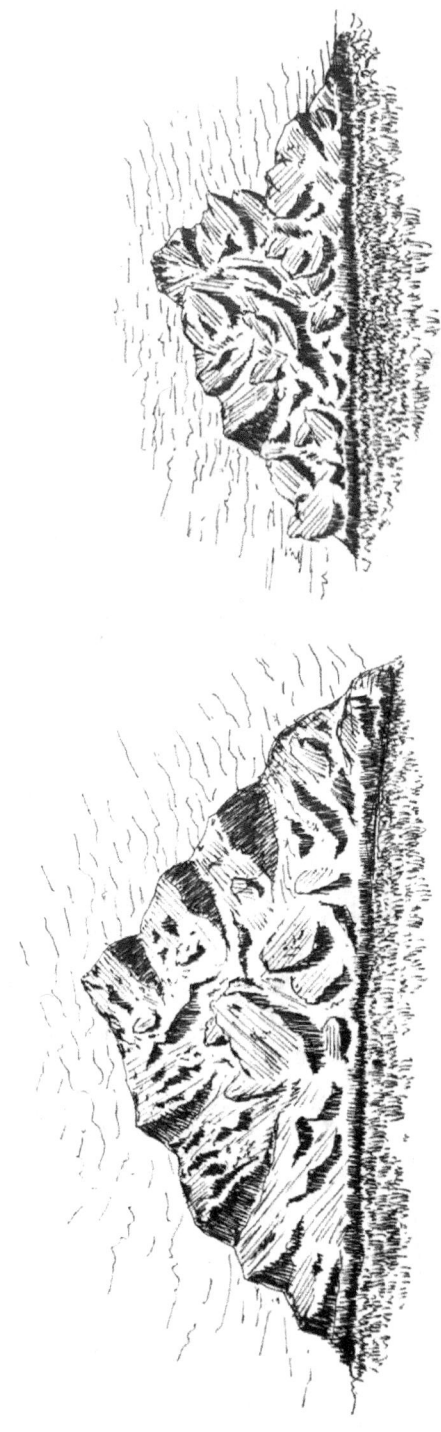

A Typical Landscape Composition:

A typical landscape with mountains will have the following elements.

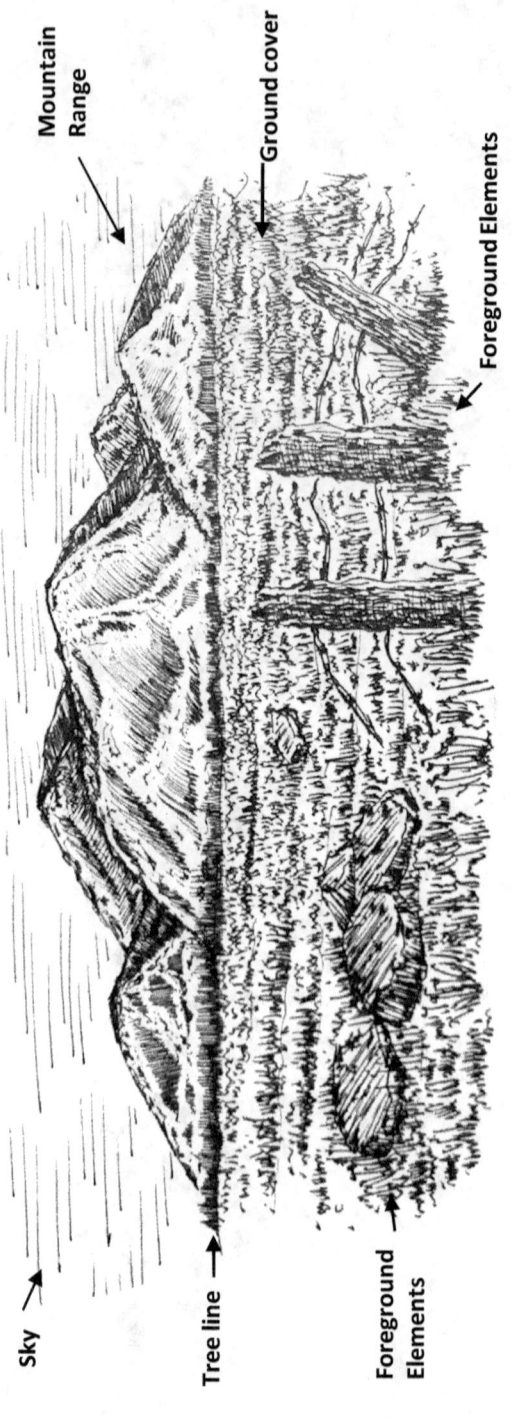

With different choices for these elements, pleasing simple landscapes can be easily drawn.

For more information visit www.pendrawings.me/getstarted

Drawing a Landscape with Mountains, Step by Step:

With following steps you can draw a pleasing mountain landscape from your imagination anytime.

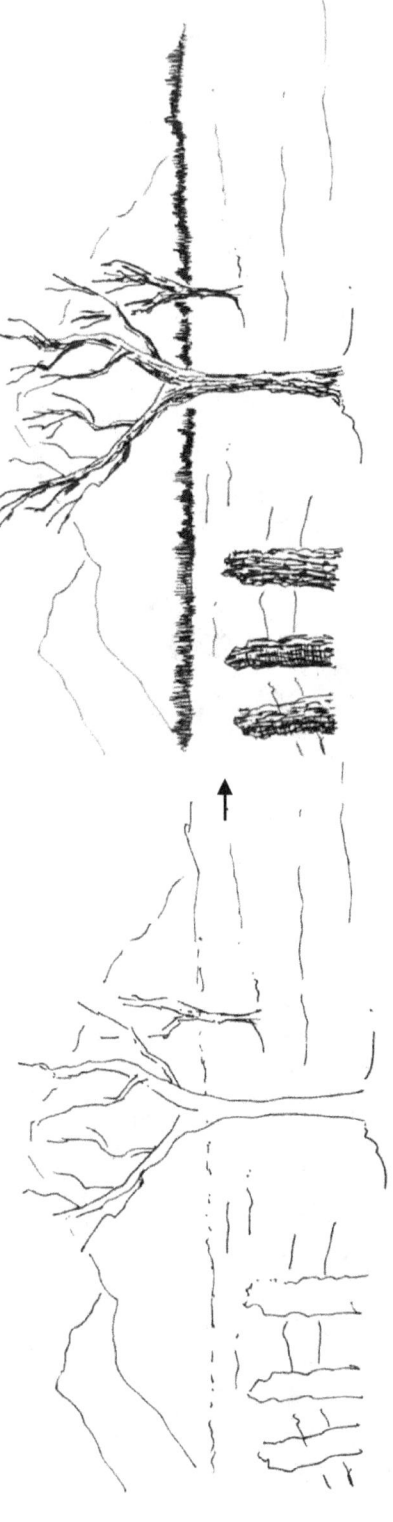

1. Draw outline. Always draw foreground elements first.

2. Texture foreground elements and distant tree line.

Drawing and texturing foreground elements like trees, posts, stones etc. is covered in detail in other volumes in this series. I encourage you to consult them as well. For more information, please visit www.pendrawings.me/workbooks

Drawing a Landscape with Mountains, Step by Step, continued:

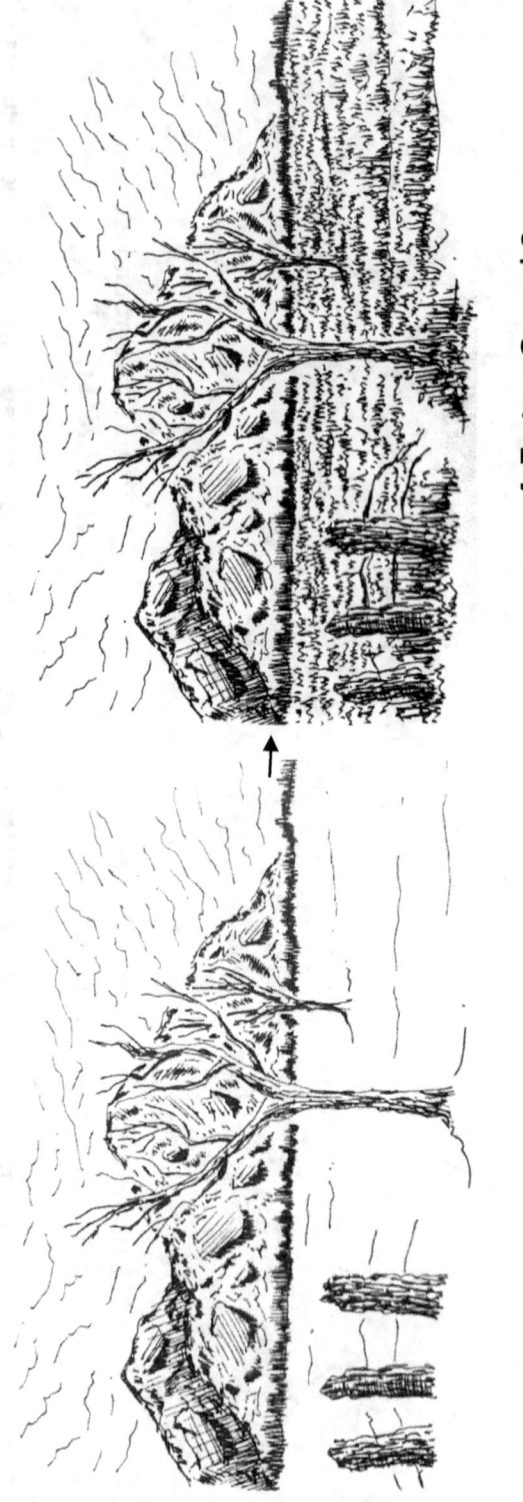

3. Texture mountains and Sky

4. Texture Ground Cover

Drawing grass and ground cover is covered in detail later.

For more information visit www.pendrawings.me/getstarted

Importance of Leaving White:

It s very important to leave some white between the elements, like between mountains and branches below, to maintain visual separation between them. In the absence of color, white provides the visual separation.

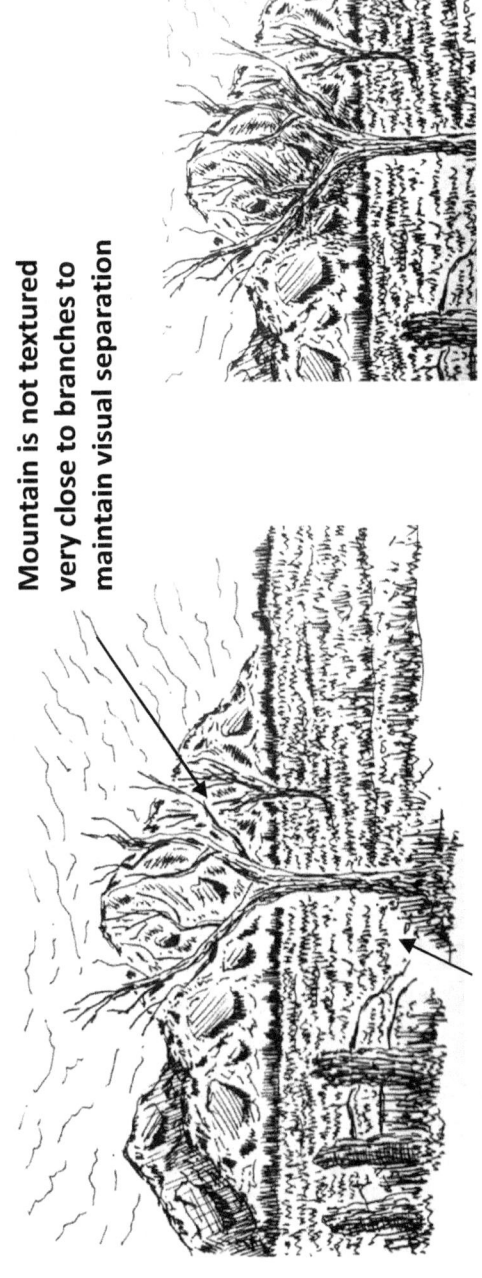

Mountain is not textured very close to branches to maintain visual separation

Grass is not textured very close to trunk and posts to maintain visual separation

Loss of visual separation is often unappealing

Try to maintain visual separation of different elements in your drawing. Experiment to see what you like.

Drawing Interesting Plains:

To make the drawing visually appealing, different 'plain lines' can be used. In this approach, instead of just being flat, the ground is made more interesting by use of plain lines as shown below.

Horizon. This is where the mountains are

Other plain lines in front of horizon

Different kind of foliage can be drawn on these lines to create visual interest

Size of foliage increases as they are drawn on plain lines closer to the viewer or away from the horizon

For more information visit www.pendrawings.me/getstarted

Drawing Foliage on Plain Lines:

Use following steps to draw foliage on the plain lines. Increase the size of foliage as it gets closer to viewer. Drawing foliage is covered in more detail in another volume of the series.

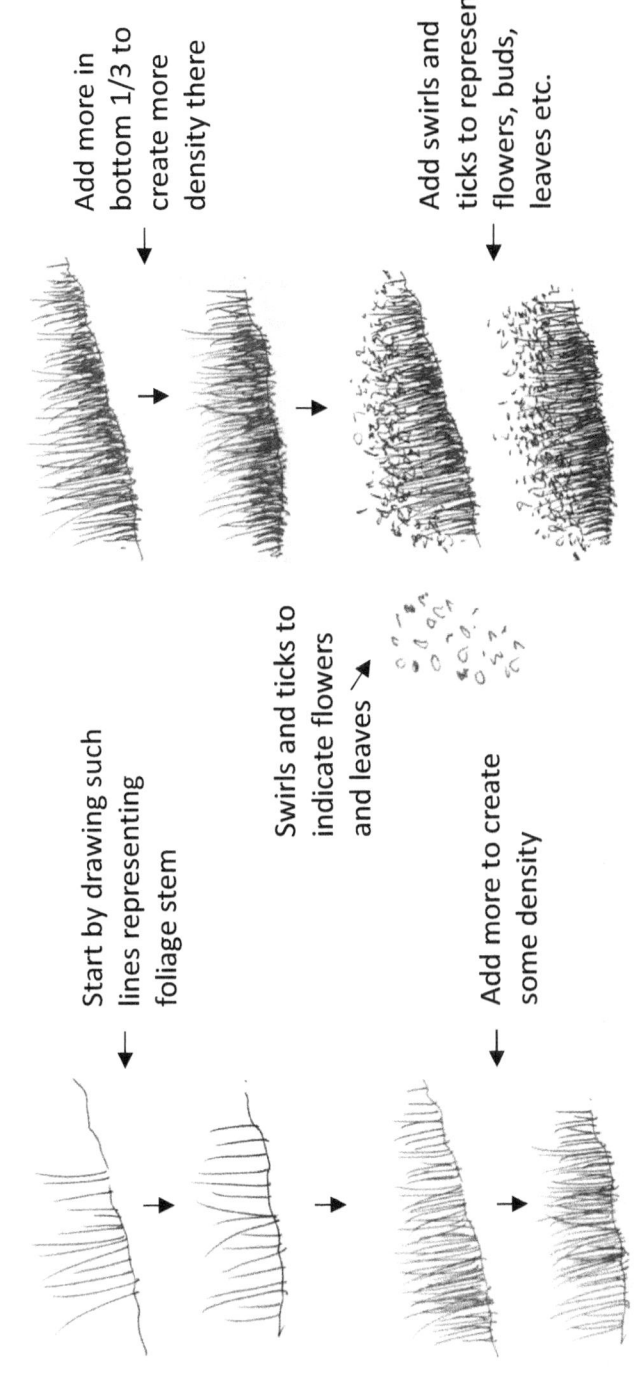

Add more in bottom 1/3 to create more density there

Add swirls and ticks to represent flowers, buds, leaves etc.

Start by drawing such lines representing foliage stem

Swirls and ticks to indicate flowers and leaves

Add more to create some density

Drawing Landscape with Interesting Ground Plains:

From horizon to foreground, plain lines are used to indicate the undulations and surface irregularities on the ground. This is visually more appealing than flat ground.

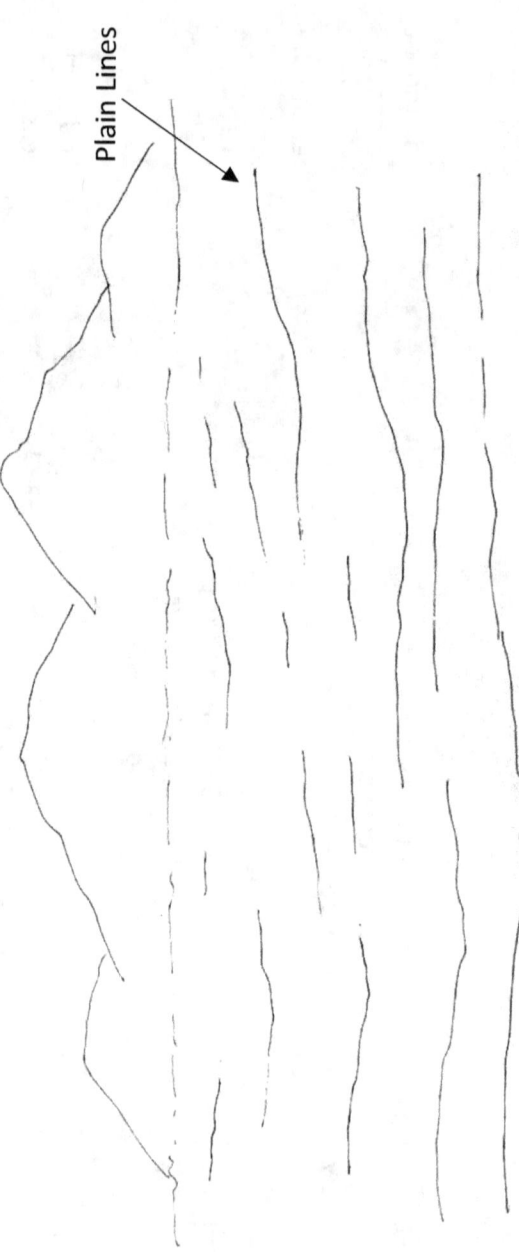

Plain Lines

Distribute the plain lines to get a sense of balance across and use interesting shapes to add visual interest. Avoid any repetition and use of simple lines.

For more information visit www.pendrawings.me/getstarted

Drawing Landscape with interesting Ground Plains, continued:

Foliage per earlier instructions is drawn on the plain lines. This brings out the ground form. Per perspective, foliage is drawn increasingly bigger as it gets closer to the viewer (away from the horizon).

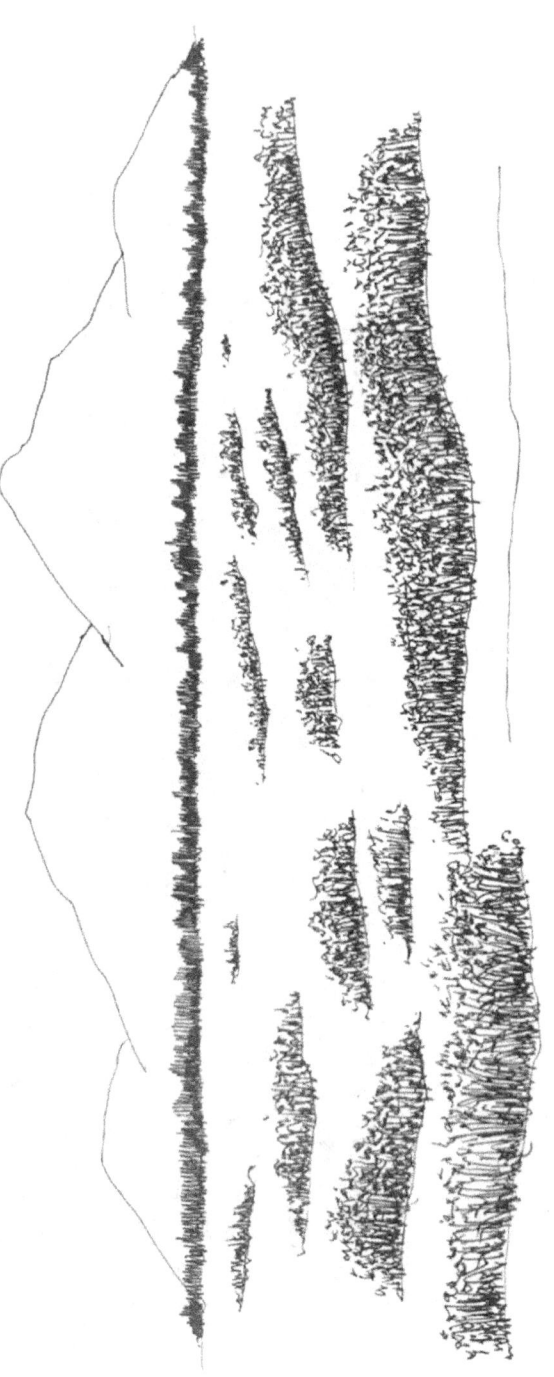

Drawing Landscape with interesting Ground Plains, continued:

Grass is added to the ground. There should be a contrast between grass and plain line foliage for it to stand out. Don't darken the grass to same level as plain line foliage. Also leave some white between top of plain foliage and grass to visually separate them.

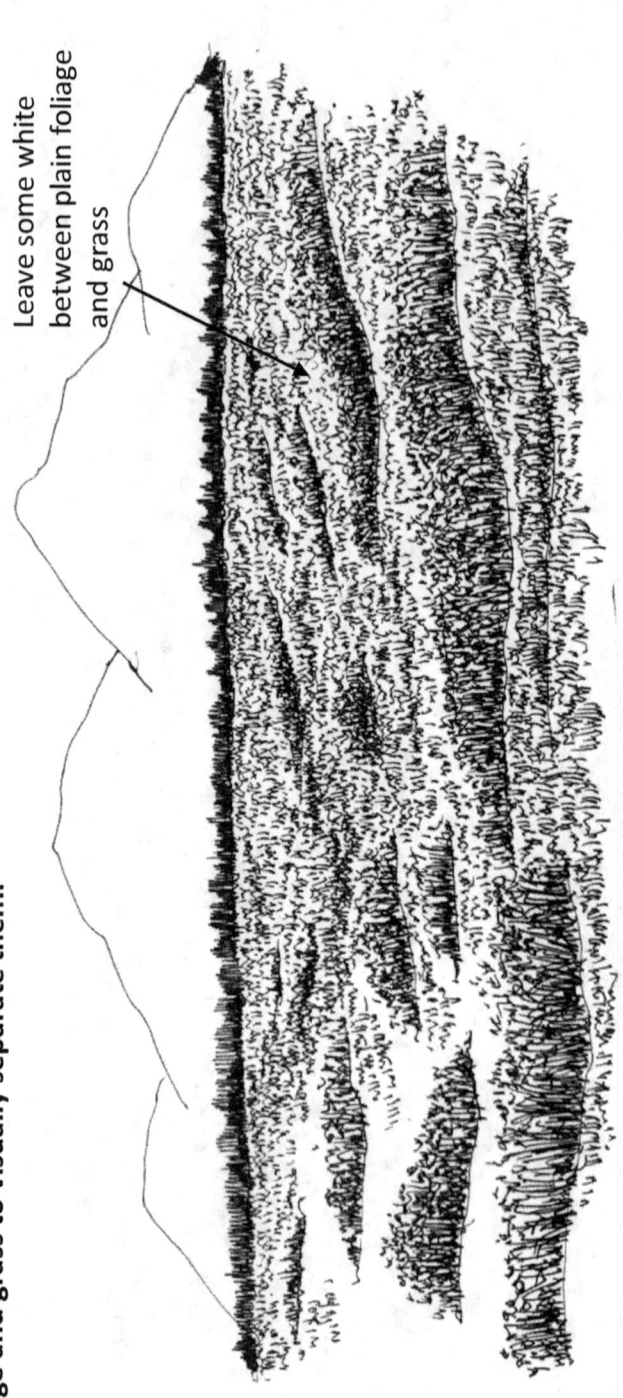

Leave some white between plain foliage and grass

Receding Pine tress in addition to foliage on the plain lines makes for a very pleasant drawing. This is discussed in another volume. Pl. visit www.pendrawings.me/workbooks for more information.

Drawing Landscape with interesting Ground Plains, continued:

Finish by drawing mountains as before. Sky/Clouds always give mountains a dramatic effect and can be added as well. Other foreground elements like stones, wooden posts, trees etc. can be added as well. They are covered in another volume in this series.

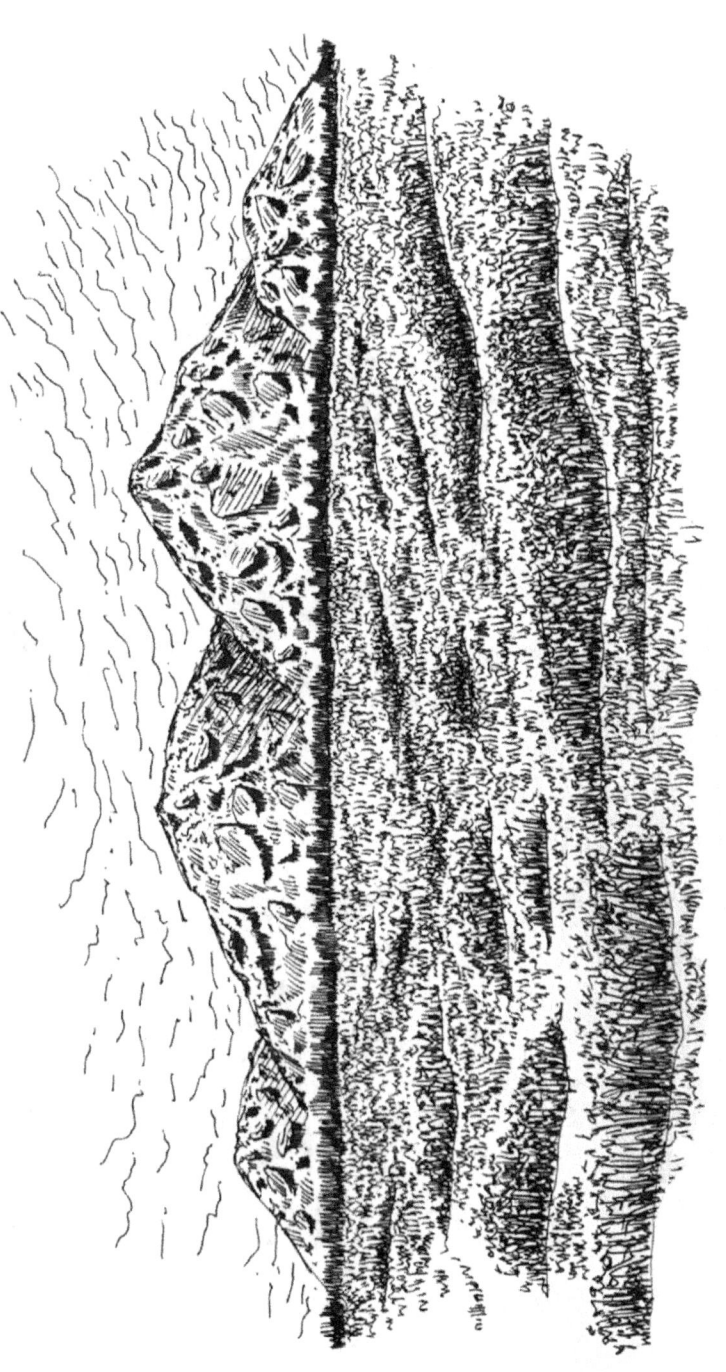

Here is another example with use of more interesting foreground elements.

More Examples of Landscape with interesting Plains:

Here are some more examples. This is a quick pleasing composition theme that can be done from your imagination anytime.

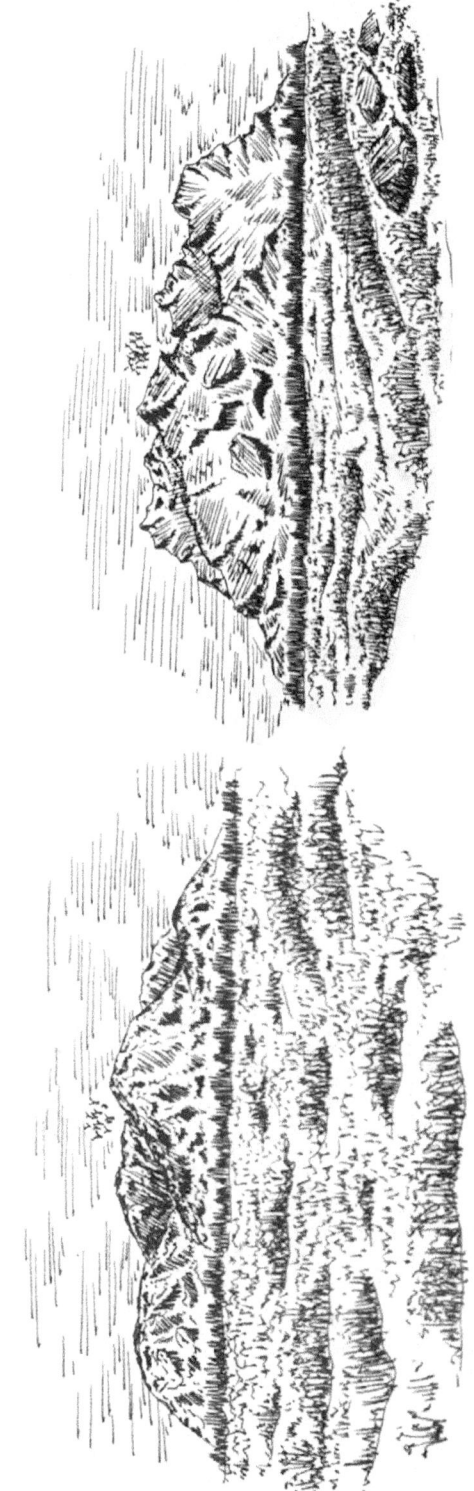

Drawing Barely Discernible Mountain:

In the previous examples, foreground elements were small and didn't hide the mountain, which allowed it to be properly textured. When using bigger foreground elements, like trees, the mountain would be mostly hidden behind them. In this case, use few big cuts and edge roughness to bring out the feel of mountains.

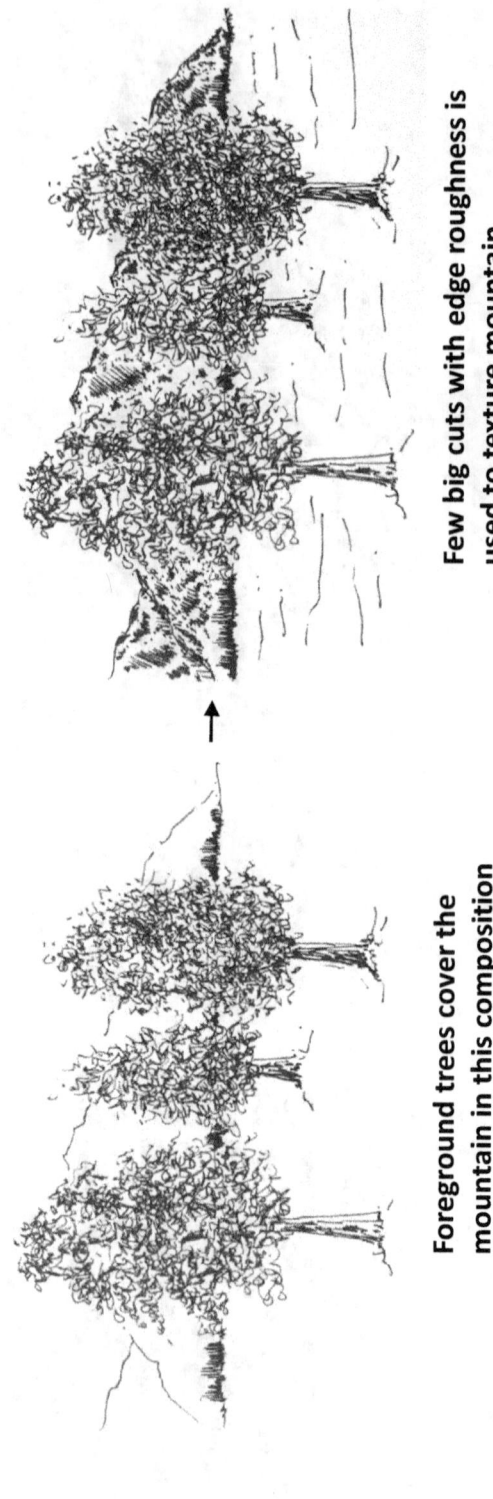

Few big cuts with edge roughness is used to texture mountain

Foreground trees cover the mountain in this composition

Avoid the temptation to over texture. In pen and ink drawing, the notion of 'suggestion' is very important. Bare suggestion of mountain with few cuts is often enough. Maintain visual separation between foreground elements and mountains.

Drawing Far Away Mountains:

Far away mountains are much smaller in size and just like barely discernible mountains in previous page, it is sufficient to 'suggest' mountain texture with few cuts. Following are some examples.

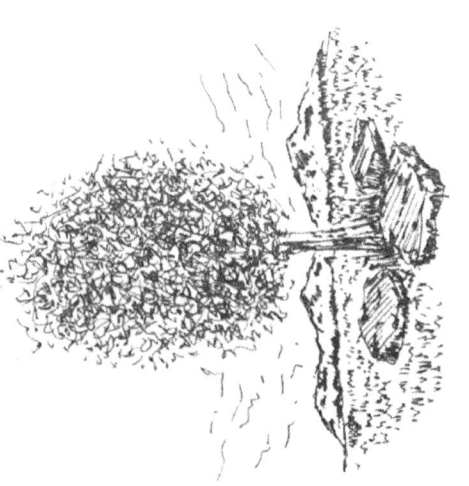

A far away mountain with a stone, wooden post or tree etc. as a foreground element is a quick simple drawing that can be attempted in short breaks.

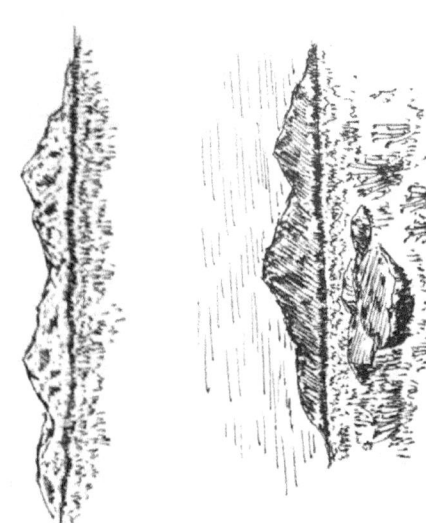

Again, avoid the temptation to over texture. In pen and ink drawing, the details are drawn in accordance with the size and closeness of an object. Far away object is smaller in size and is draw with less details than a closer object.

For more information visit www.pendrawings.me/getstarted

Drawing Mountain Range:

A mountain range can be drawn in a manner similar to drawing a mountain keeping following 3 important points in mind.

1. Always start by drawing mountains in front and then proceed backwards.
2. Make the mountains smaller as they go out due to perspective.
3. Make the base of mountains behind slightly darker.

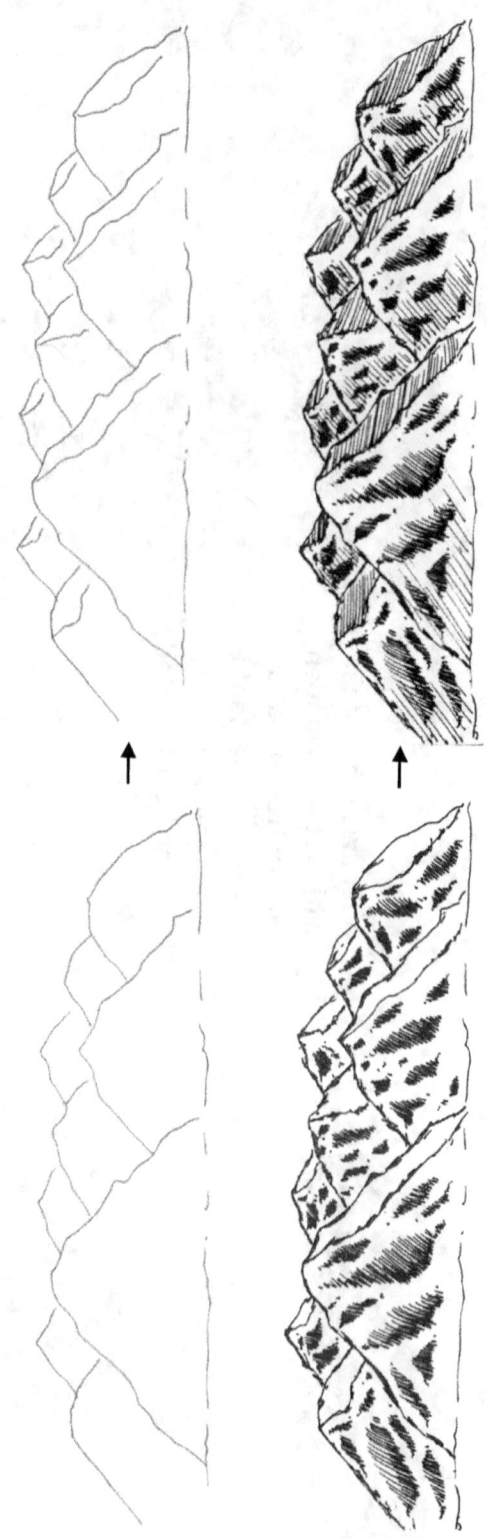

Continued on next page

Drawing Mountain Range, Continued:

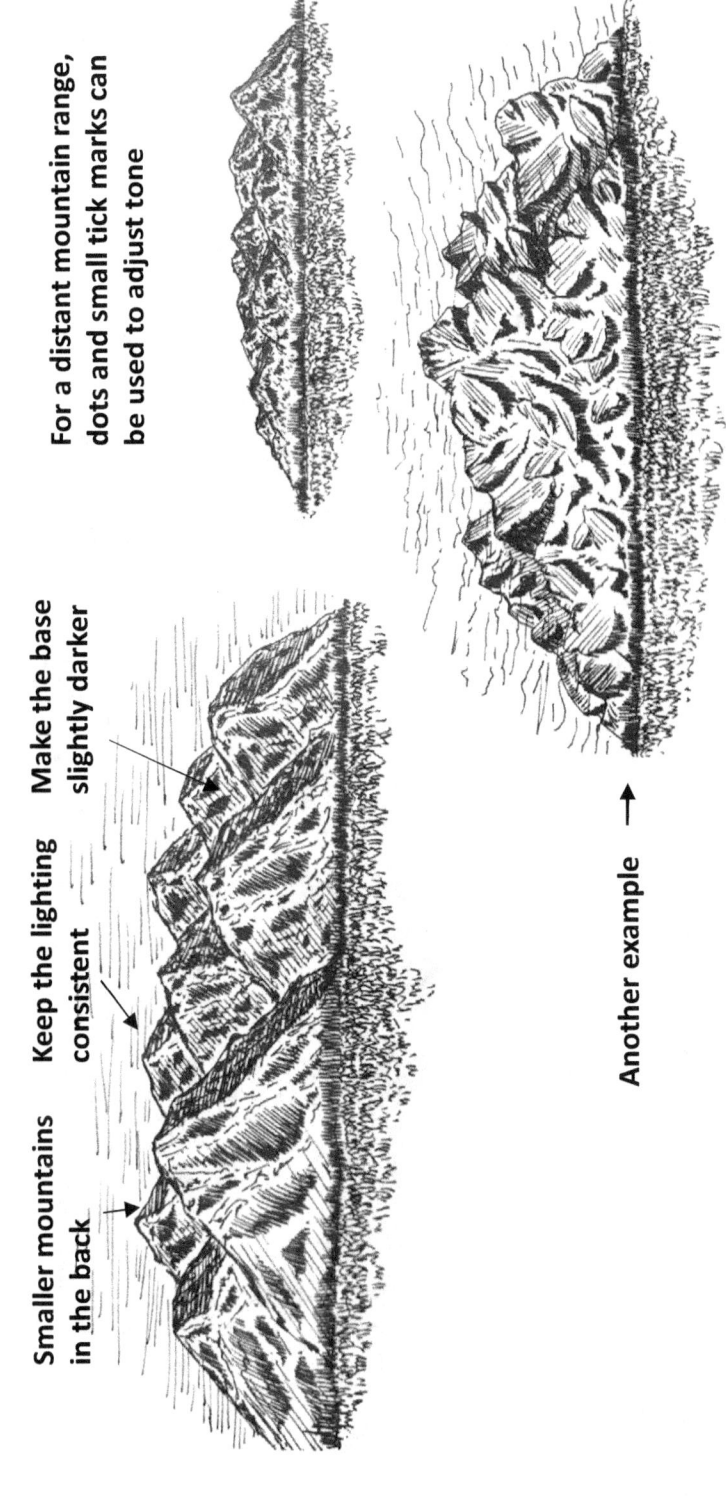

For a distant mountain range, dots and small tick marks can be used to adjust tone

Smaller mountains in the back

Keep the lighting consistent

Make the base slightly darker

Another example →

For more information visit www.pendrawings.me/getstarted

Importance of Tonal Difference in a Mountain Range:

To distinguish between different mountains in a mountain range, it is important to make the base of mountains in the back darker as shown below.

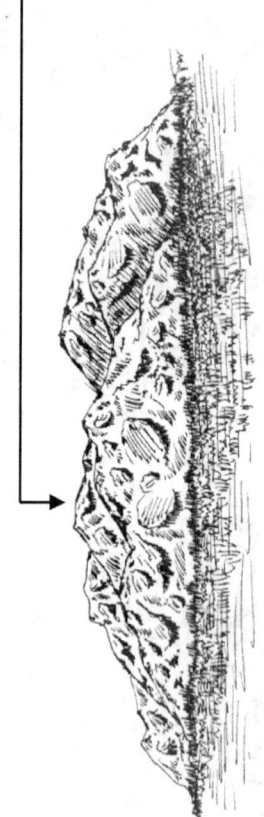

Without the difference in tone, successive ranges don't stand out and blend into each other

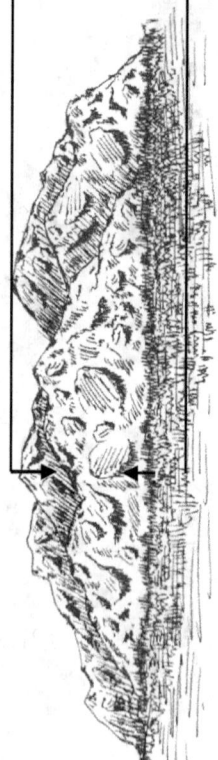

By darkening the base of successive mountains and leaving their top lighter, they stand out

Base of mountain in front can be darkened as well though it is not necessary to do so

For more information visit www.pendrawings.me/getstarted

Distant Element on Base of Mountain:

A distant element, like a tree line, on the base of mountain is usually pleasing. I have used it in drawings so far. It can be easily drawn using vertical parallel lines as shown below .

Use undulating vertical lines likes these to indicate a distant tree line

To give more depth, base can be made darker in an irregular manner. This creates two layer of distant tree line.

For more information visit www.pendrawings.me/getstarted

Distant Element on Base of Mountain, Continued:

To make distant tree line more interesting, more layers can be used. Use tonal difference between successive layers to create more depth in distant tree line.

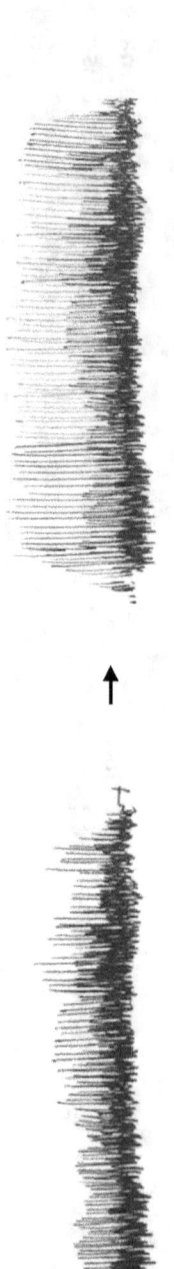

Another layer of vertical parallel lines is added.

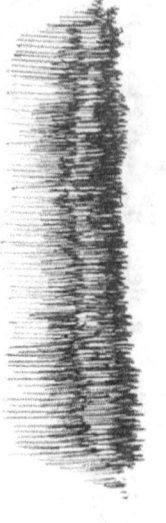

Middle layer can be slightly darkened to further brink it out. There should be a sliver of lighter tone between layers for them to stand apart.

For more information visit www.pendrawings.me/getstarted

Activity: Drawing Distant Element

Practice drawing layers of Distant Element below per earlier instructions.

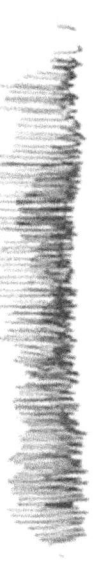

Layers of Distant Elements, Examples:

In the following mountains that we have seen before, I have extended their simple base tree line with another layer. This gives it more visual interest.

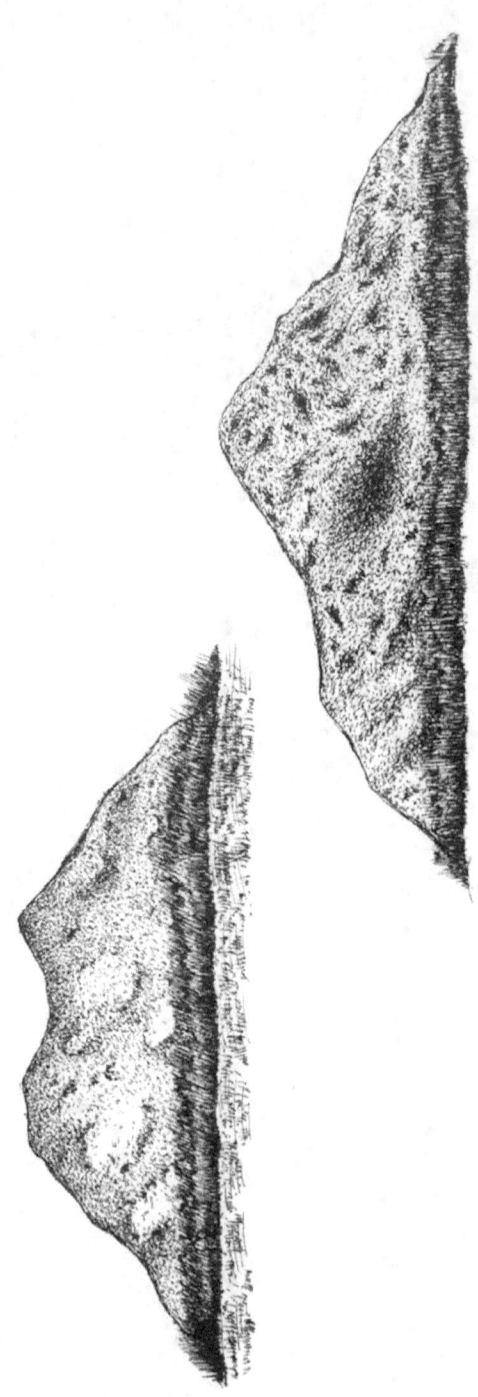

Notice that there should be a sliver of lighter tone between the layers to make them stand apart. Also successive layers on the top should have relative lighter tone. Keep the texturing of mountain lighter around the tree line to keep the appearance clean.

Drawing a Hill:

Just like a mountain, a distant hill also provides a nice backdrop to a drawing. A distant hill can be drawn using the following stroke, which is similar to drawing a distant grass. This gives an appearance of distant grass covered hill.

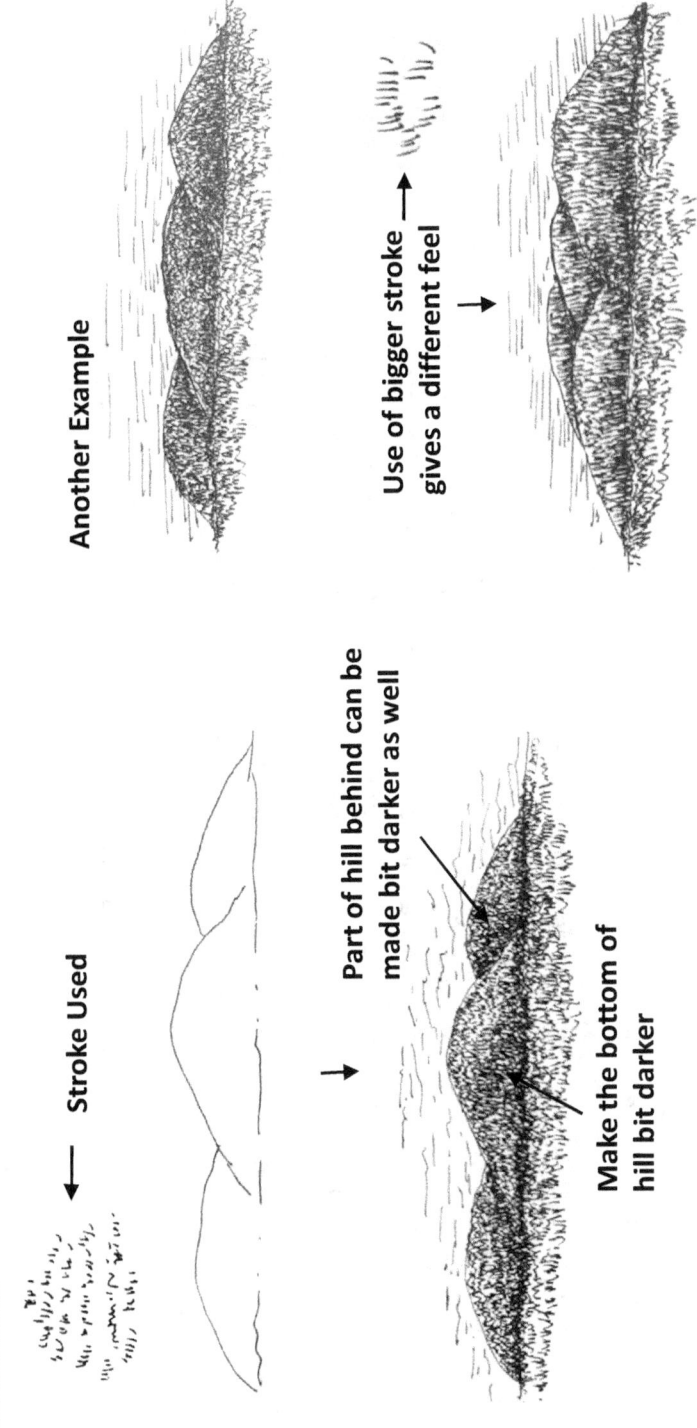

Stroke Used

Another Example

Part of hill behind can be made bit darker as well

Make the bottom of hill bit darker

Use of bigger stroke gives a different feel

Drawing Grass and Ground Cover:

Ground is part of any landscape and providing some kind of ground cover on the ground always makes a drawing visually appealing. We have seen many examples of use of grass for ground cover earlier and in next few pages, you will learn how to draw it.

Though the stroke for grass is quite simple, to get a good feel for it, it is very important to drawn it in a 'random' manner. If a specific pattern emerges, then it will be quickly caught by our eyes and destroy the intended effect as grass in nature is never in a 'pattern'. To accomplish this, keep you hand moving. Draw few strokes of grass in one corner and then move on to another corner and then to another area. Hand movement like this will help you avoid drawing in a pattern.

Also the notion of 'suggestion' is very important when drawing grass. Usually few strokes of grass can convey the right feel and it is not necessary to cover the whole ground with grass stroke. Experiment with different levels to see what you prefer.

It is also important to maintain visual separation between different elements in a pen and ink drawing by leaving a thin layer of white between them. When drawing grass, it is especially important to maintain such distinction between grass and foreground elements. That said, the intensity of grass can itself be varied to make it more interesting as explained in following pages.

Drawing Ground Cover:

Almost all landscapes need some ground cover. Grass and wild flowers are very easy to draw and provide a great way to add interest in any drawing. Ground cover is drawn from horizon line to the foreground

Stroke for distant grass magnified

Horizon Line

Stroke for middle ground grass magnified

For distant grass, simply use small tick marks or 'wriggles' '

This is the basic stroke to draw grass. Notice that lines are NOT parallel but slightly curved with a 'root'

Just like other elements, grass decreases in size as it goes out in the distance

As you get closer, draw bigger grass using grass stroke

Don't use straight vertical lines

Avoid regular pattern

for more information visit www.pendrawings.me/getstarted

Drawing Ground Cover Continued:

Continued from previous page.

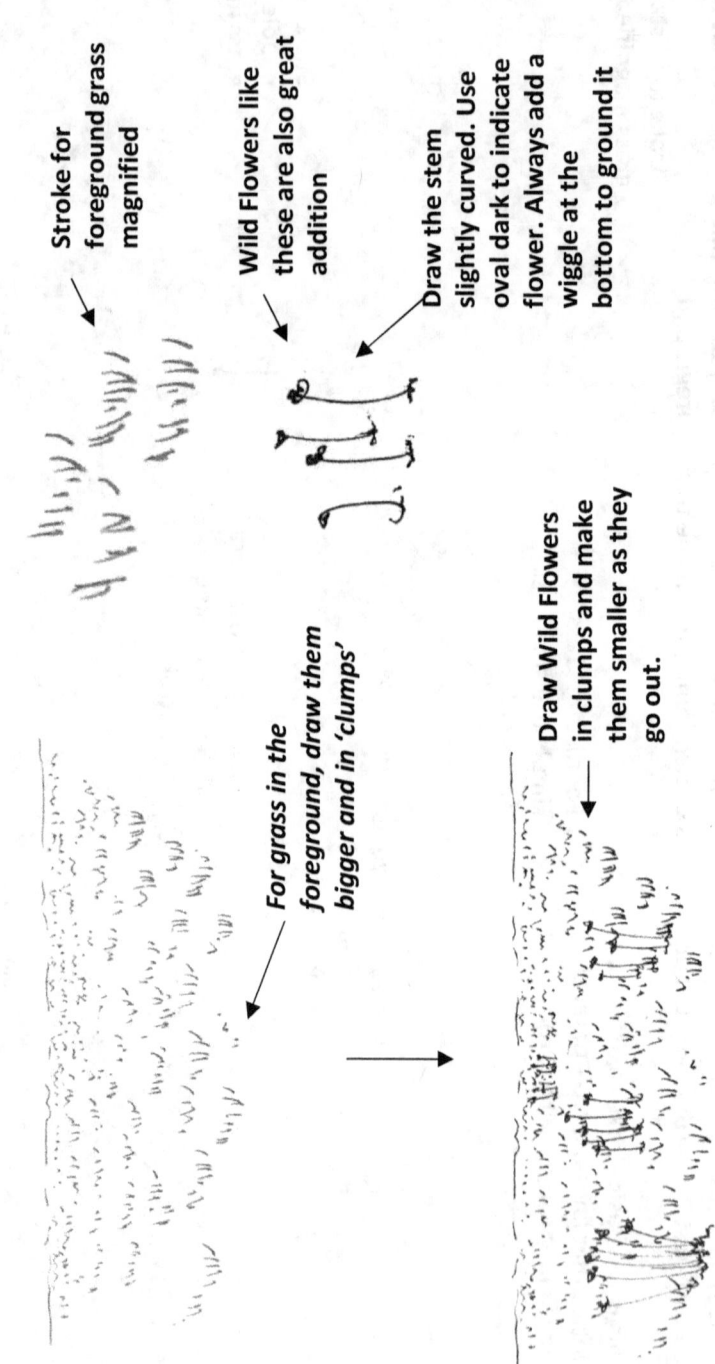

Stroke for foreground grass magnified

Wild Flowers like these are also great addition

Draw the stem slightly curved. Use oval dark to indicate flower. Always add a wiggle at the bottom to ground it

For grass in the foreground, draw them bigger and in 'clumps'

Draw Wild Flowers in clumps and make them smaller as they go out.

For more information visit www.pendrawings.me/getstarted

Relative intensity of ground cover:

Just some grass stroke is enough to give a feel of ground cover. Often explicit covering of all ground with grass is not needed. But more density of grass can be used to create different feel if needed.

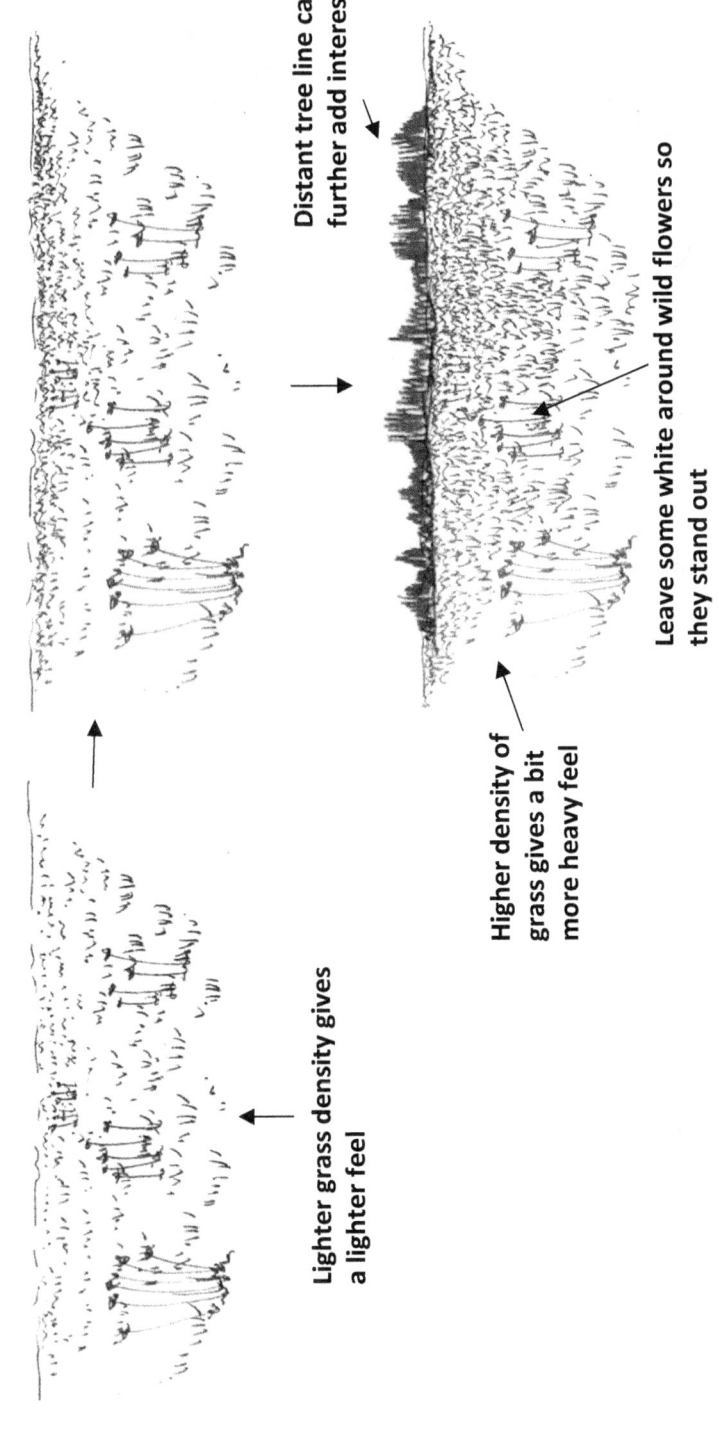

Lighter grass density gives a lighter feel

Higher density of grass gives a bit more heavy feel

Distant tree line can further add interest

Leave some white around wild flowers so they stand out

Activity: Drawing ground cover:

Draw grass and a distant element per earlier instructions below. Draw ground cover for earlier activities as well.

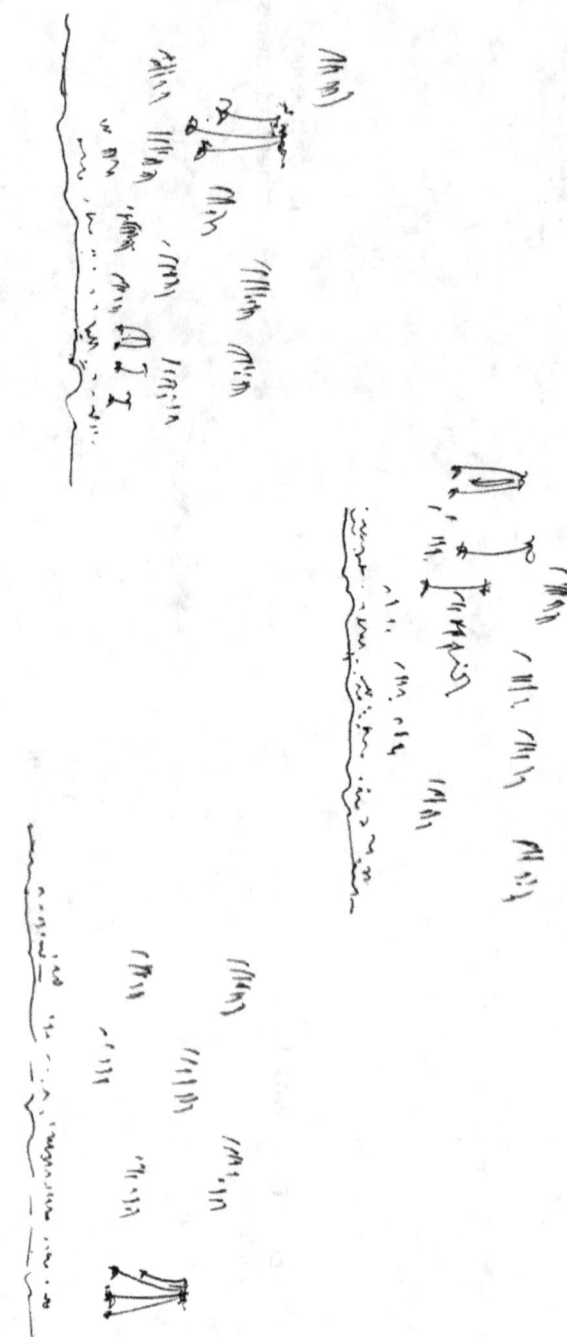

For more information visit www.pendrawings.me/getstarted

Drawing Water:

Addition of Water can make any drawing more visually interesting. Believable depiction of reflections in water is key to drawing it successfully. Water can be either still or in turbulence and can be either flowing across or towards a viewer. Different techniques are required to draw water in different states and these are covered next.

State of reflection of an object in water indicates the movement of water. In still water, the reflection has no distortion and the edges are sharp and almost has a feel of mirror. As the movement of water picks up, the reflections start to get distorted and the edges become hazy. The level of distortion of reflection indicates the level of water movement or turbulence.

There are many technical aspects to consider when drawing reflection in water of an object and not all are covered in next few pages. The aim instead is to show how quick simple drawings incorporating water can be done using simple foreground elements like posts, trees, stones etc. Such simple pleasing drawings can be done relatively quickly and easily after water stroke and related techniques are understood and practiced.

Drawing Still Water:

Water is essentially indicated by the presence of reflection of an object. Reflection can be drawn in various ways as discussed next. When reflection is combined with 'water stroke', a feeling of water is obtained.

Drawing Still Water:

Parallel Line is used to draw reflection

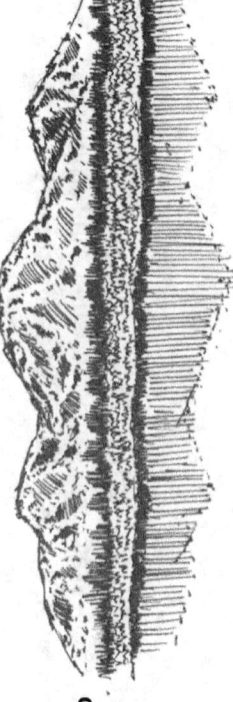

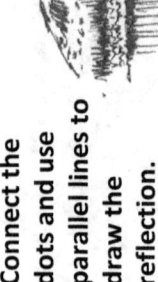

Start by putting dots to represent the high and low points of the mountain.

Connect the dots and use parallel lines to draw the reflection.

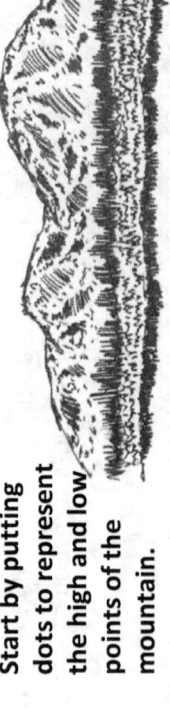

Water flowing across can be depicted using this stroke. Each lines indicates a very small ripple of water and together with reflection, it gives a feel of water.

In still water, edges of reflection are well defined. As the turbulence in water increases, edges of reflection gets distorted.

For more information visit www.pendrawings.me/getstarted

Drawing Still Water, continued:

The shape of reflection doesn't have to 'fully' match the object but it should convey the same 'feel' with same high and low points. Our eyes are very perceptible to overall shape and this should be consistent in the reflection.

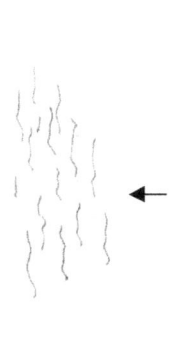

Water flowing across can be depicted using this stroke. Each lines indicates a very small ripple of water and together with reflection, it gives a feel of water.

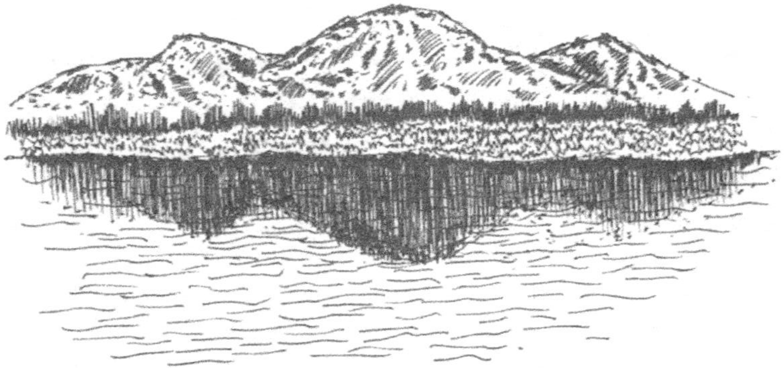

The tone of reflection should match the tone of object, but it is usually difficult to do so in an object like mountains with varied tone. In this case an overall darker tone gives best impression.

Darken the reflection more using another set of parallel lines.

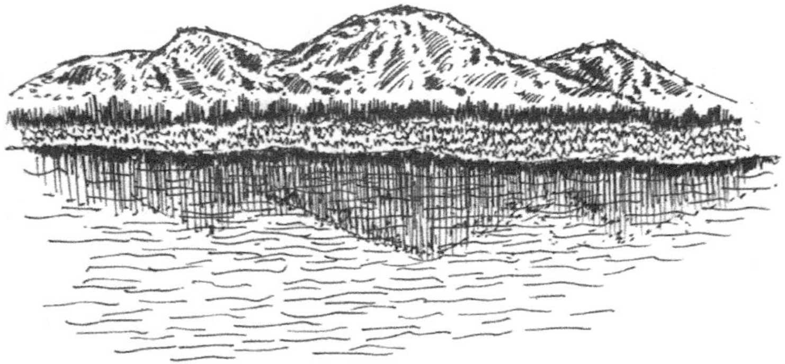

Reflection can be further darkened to give more intense feel.

Activity Drawing Still Water:

Add reflections to the following per earlier instructions. Draw some of your own.

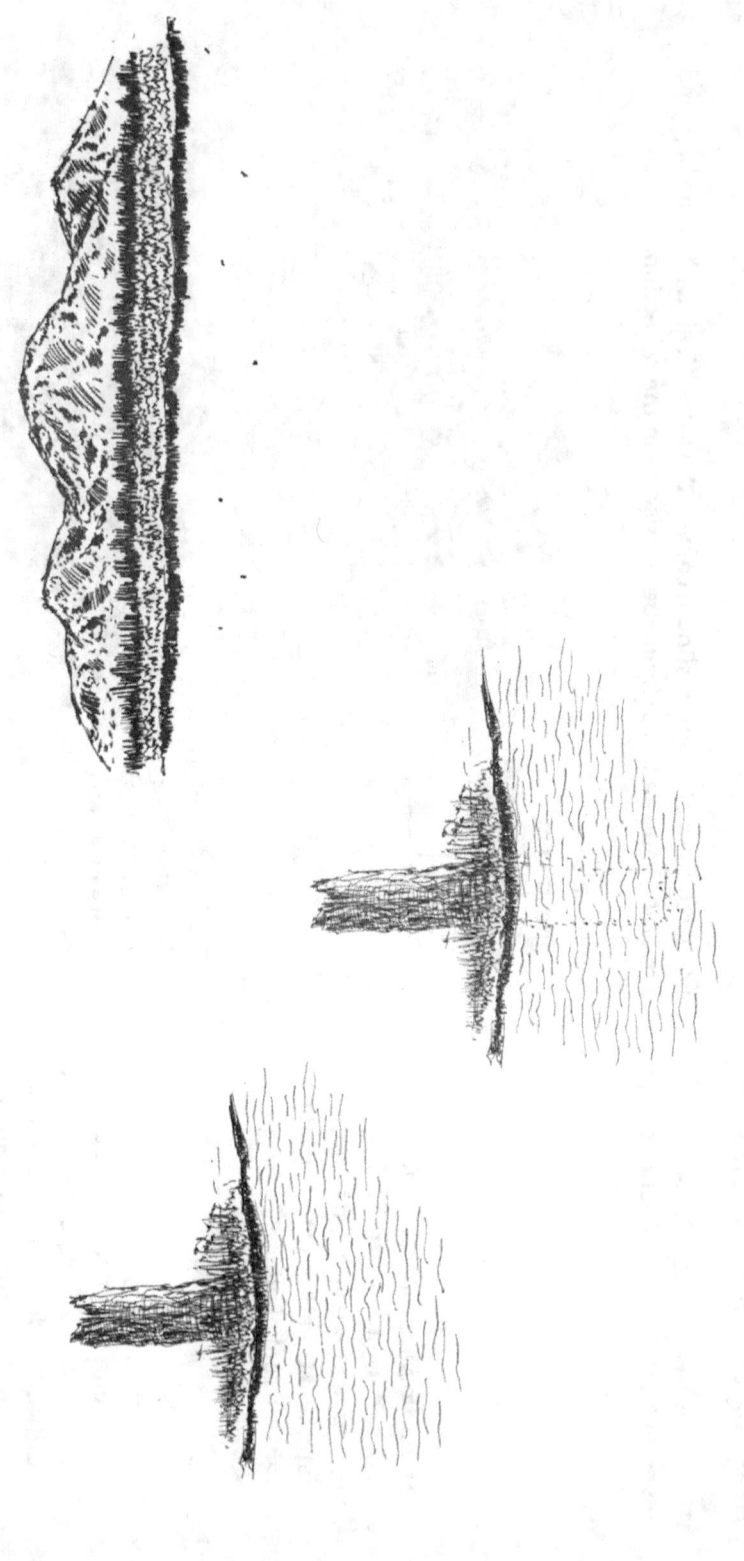

Drawing Still Reflection:

In a still reflection the shape and size of object and reflection must closely match. Unless the object is simple, it is usually difficult to do. Choose either an object with unique shape or feature that is part of reflection as well and hence makes the still reflection believable, or else, for objects with more interesting shapes, choose more turbulent reflection (discussed next), where the reflection has to be approximate.

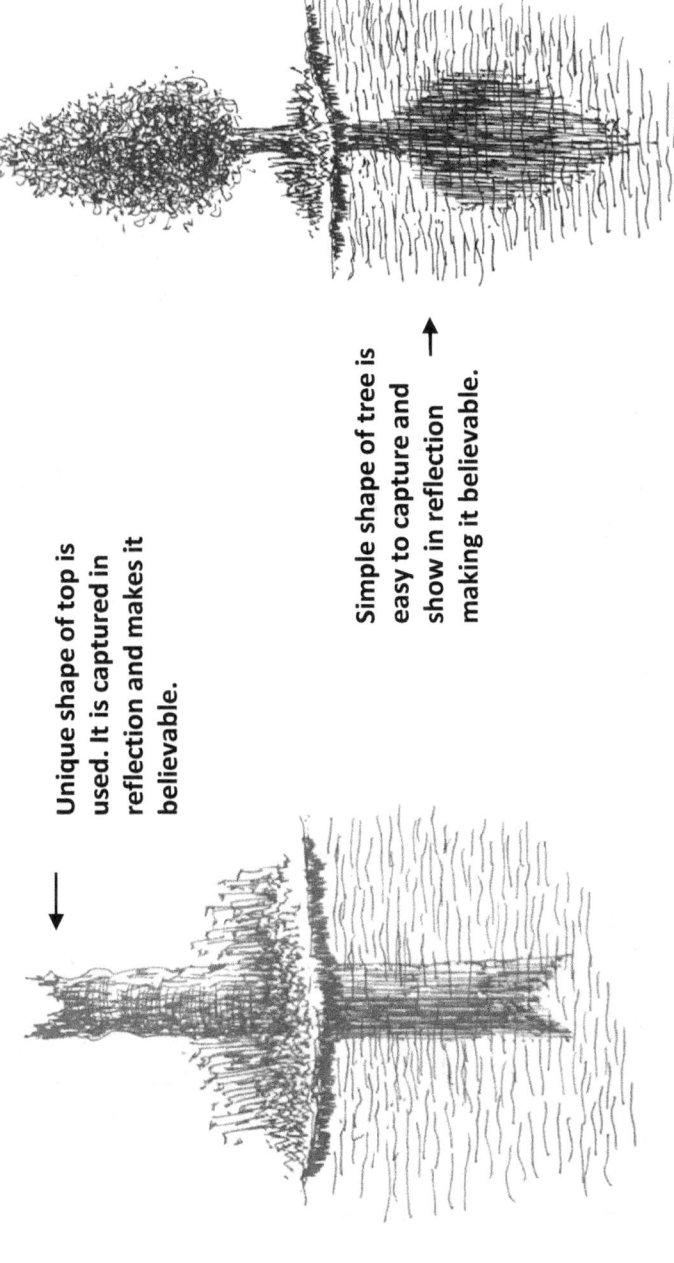

Unique shape of top is used. It is captured in reflection and makes it believable.

Simple shape of tree is easy to capture and show in reflection making it believable.

For more information visit www.perdrawings.me/getstarted

Drawing Turbulent Water:

To draw turbulent water, reflection is distorted. In this technique, reflection is drawn using more layers of water stroke. Horizontal hatching lines can be used to darken reflection as well

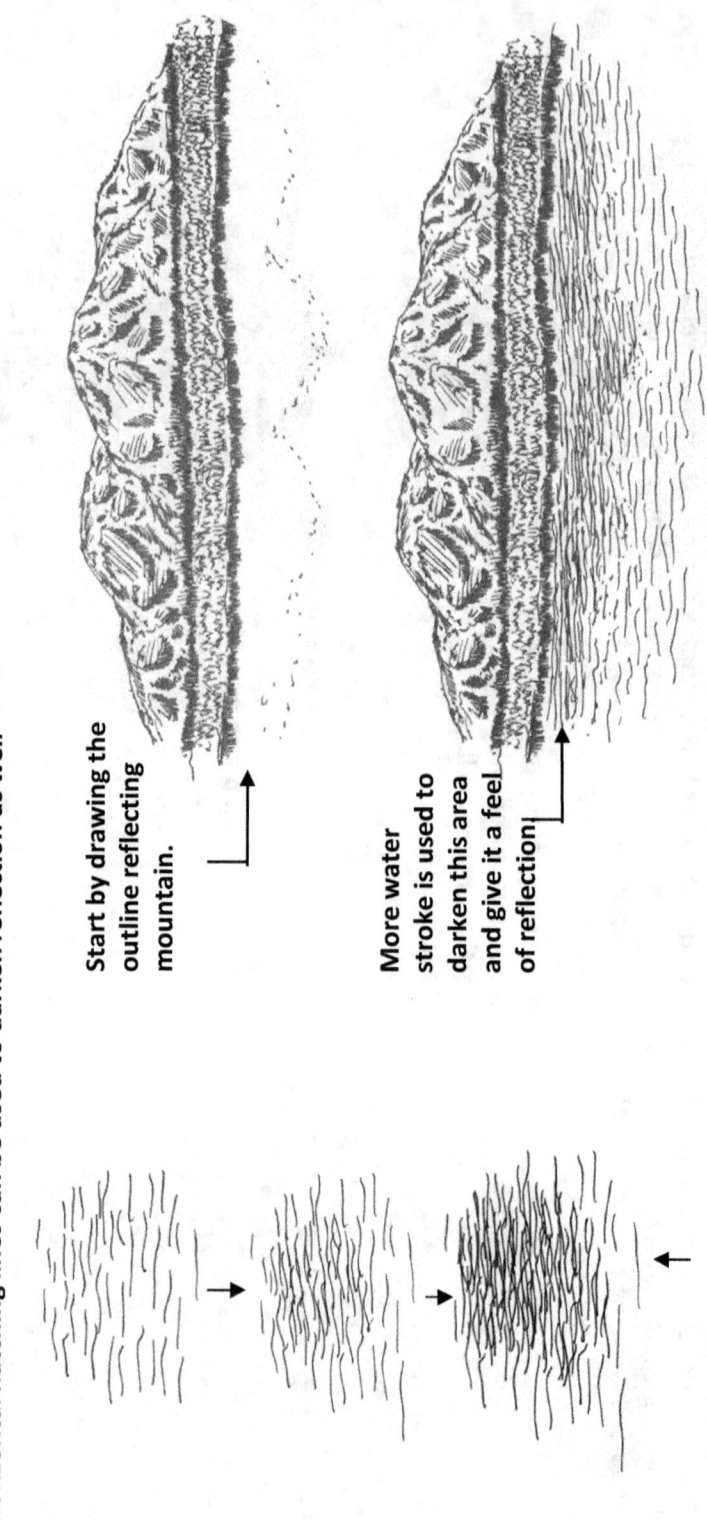

Start by drawing the outline reflecting mountain.

More water stroke is used to darken this area and give it a feel of reflection.

Reflection doesn't have well defined edge which gives an indication of more water movement (turbulence).

In this techniques, more water stroke is used to indicate darker tone (reflection).

For more information visit www.pendrawings.me/getstarted

Relative Intensity of Reflection:

Intensity of reflection can be adjusted per taste. Darker reflection gives more intense and foreboding feeling where as lighter reflection is more suitable when reflection doesn't have to stand out.

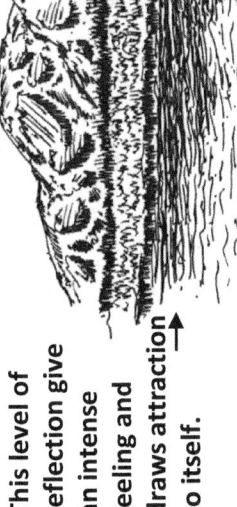

More darker reflection than last page. This level is sufficient for most usage.

This level of reflection give an intense feeling and draws attraction to itself.

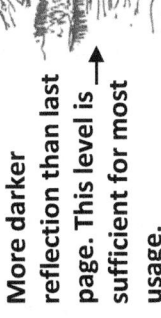

Well defined edges with vertical line

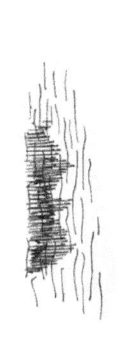

Unlike well defined edges in still reflection using parallel lines, for turbulent water, additional water stroke and horizontal lines are used to create a slightly fuzzy edge giving it feel of water movement or turbulence.

More Examples of Reflection:

Following are some more examples of water reflection. Study them and use the tips mentioned in your own attempts.

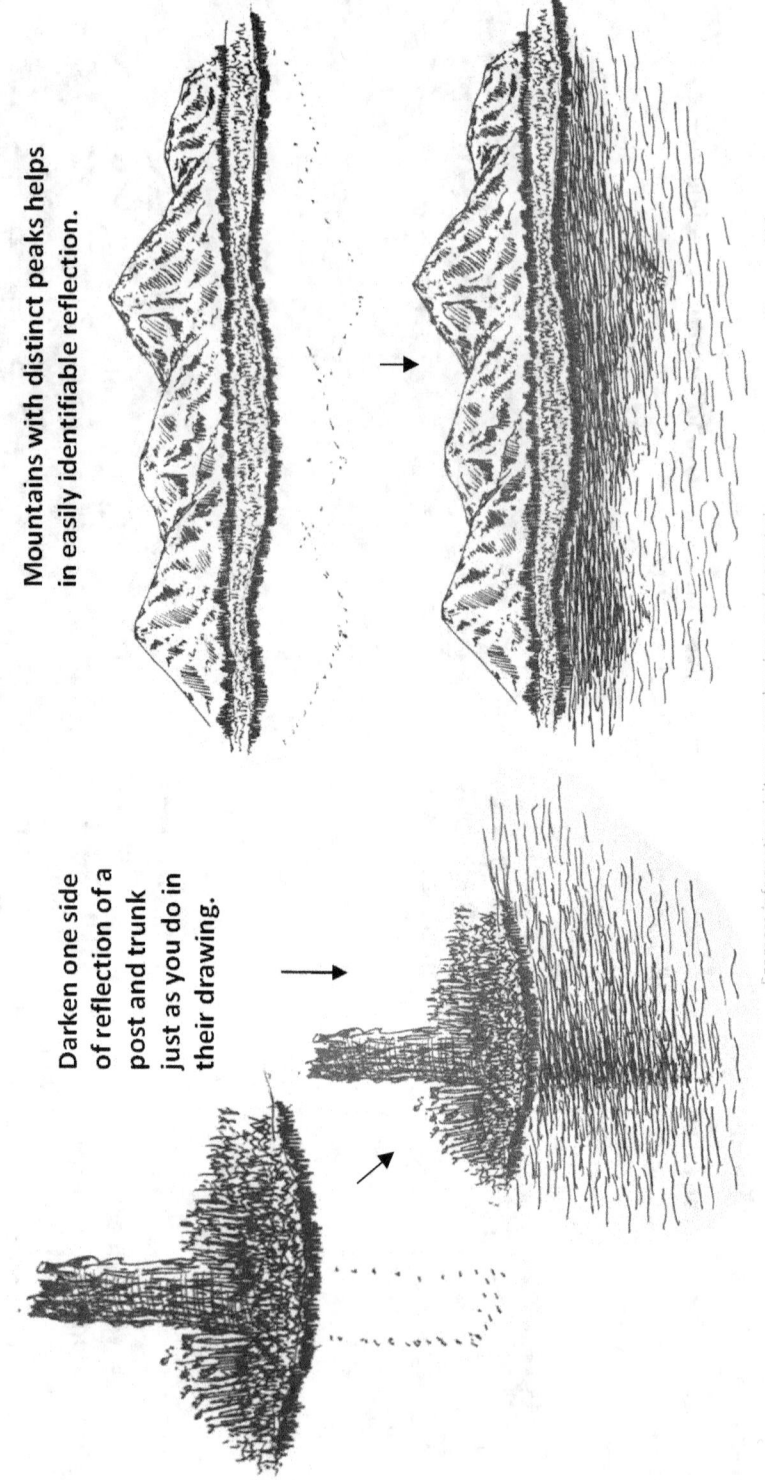

Mountains with distinct peaks helps in easily identifiable reflection.

Darken one side of reflection of a post and trunk just as you do in their drawing.

For more information visit www.pendrawings.me/getstarted

More Examples of Reflection:

Following are some more examples of water reflection. Study them and use the tips mentioned in your own attempts.

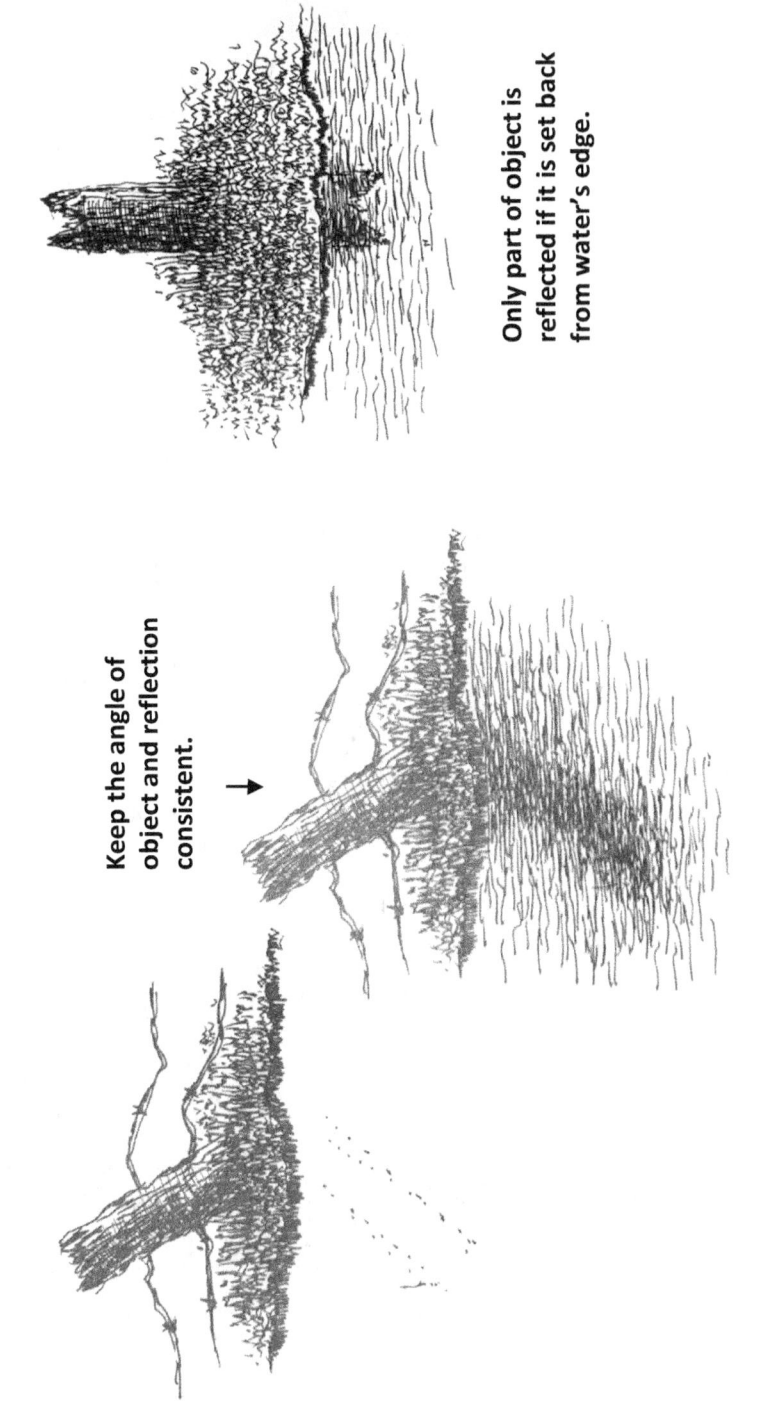

Keep the angle of object and reflection consistent.

Only part of object is reflected if it is set back from water's edge.

For more information visit www.pendrawings.me/getstarted

More Examples of Reflection:

Following are some more examples of water reflection. Study them and use the tips mentioned in your own attempts.

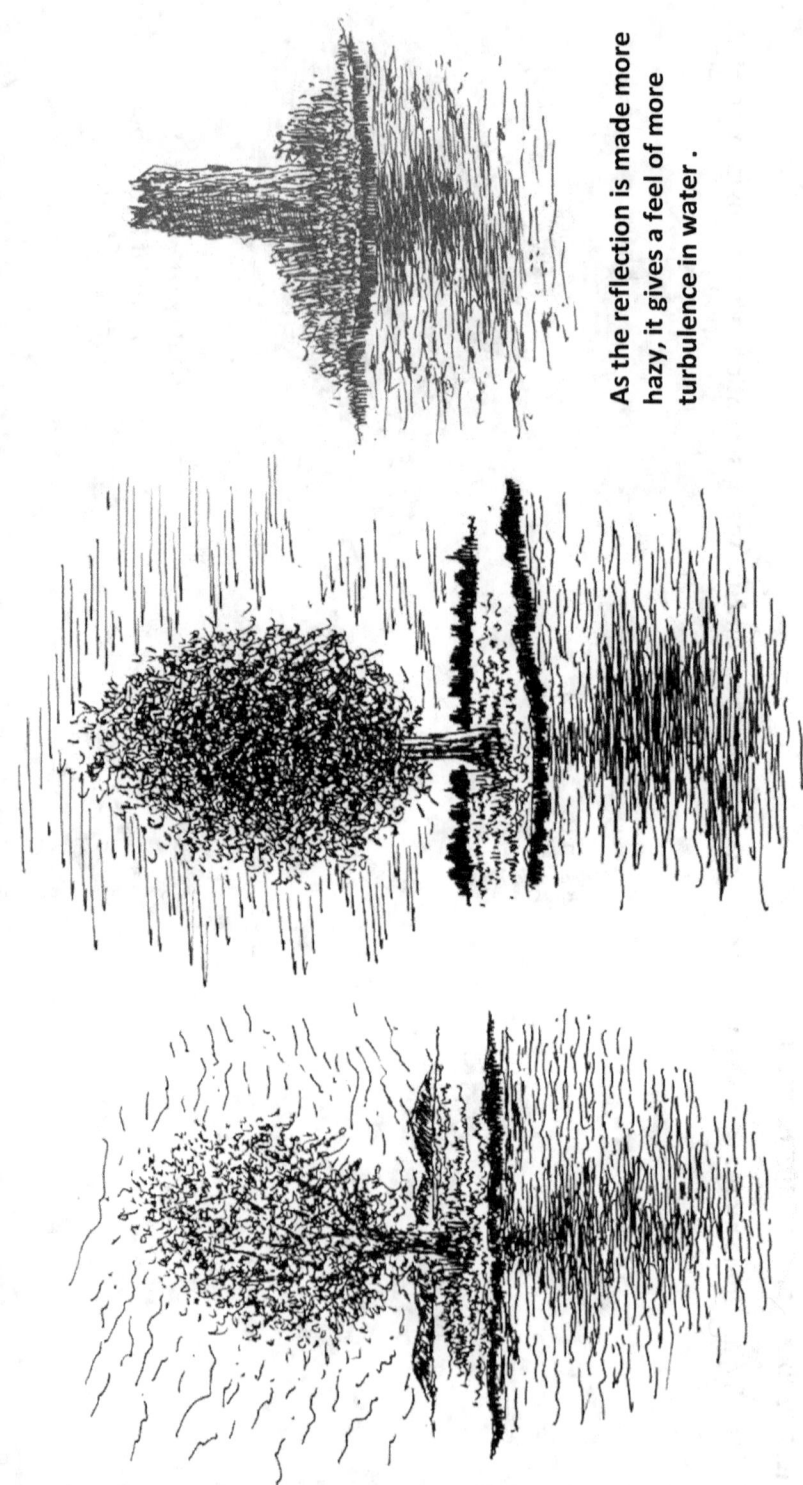

As the reflection is made more hazy, it gives a feel of more turbulence in water .

More Examples of Reflection:

A group of stones in water is a simple pleasing drawing that can be quickly enjoyed any time. Drawing stones is covered in detail in another volume. Pl. visit www.pendrawings.me/workbooks for information on other volumes.

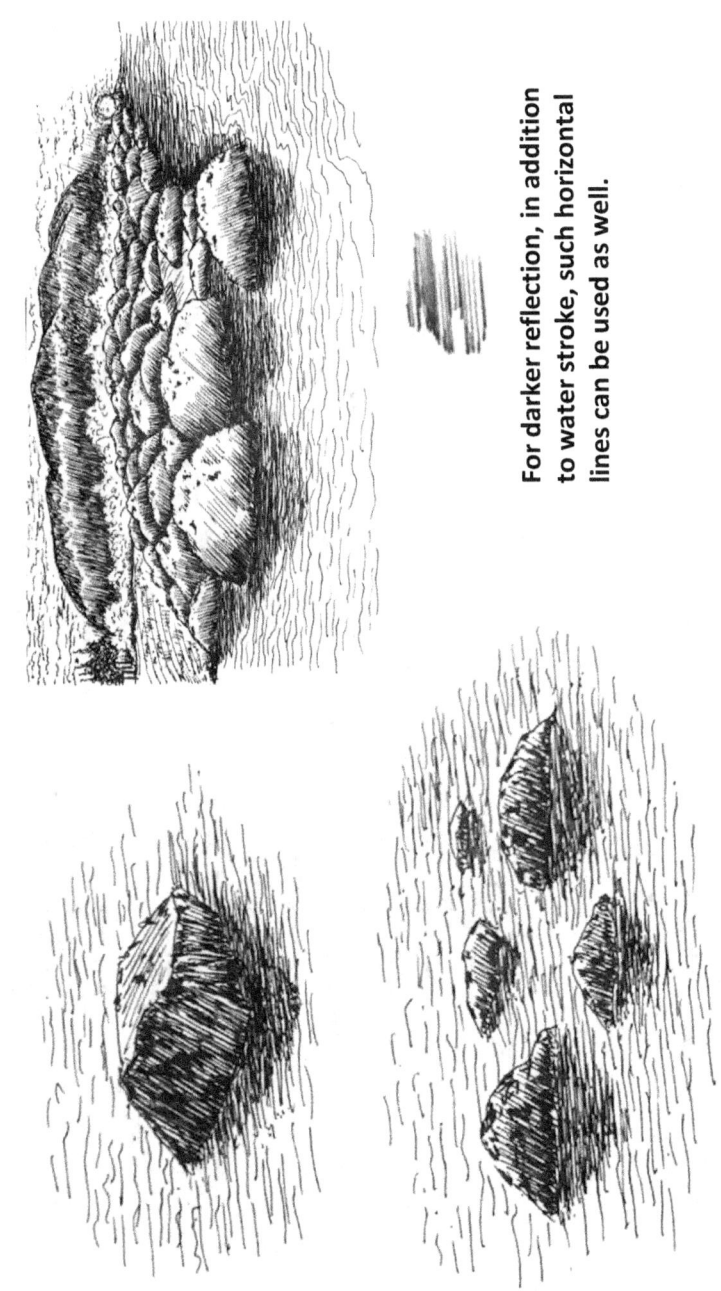

For darker reflection, in addition to water stroke, such horizontal lines can be used as well.

Landscapes with Water:

In most compositions with water, it is indicated in the front with appropriate reflection as seen in examples so far. Here is a landscape that was earlier discussed with addition of water.

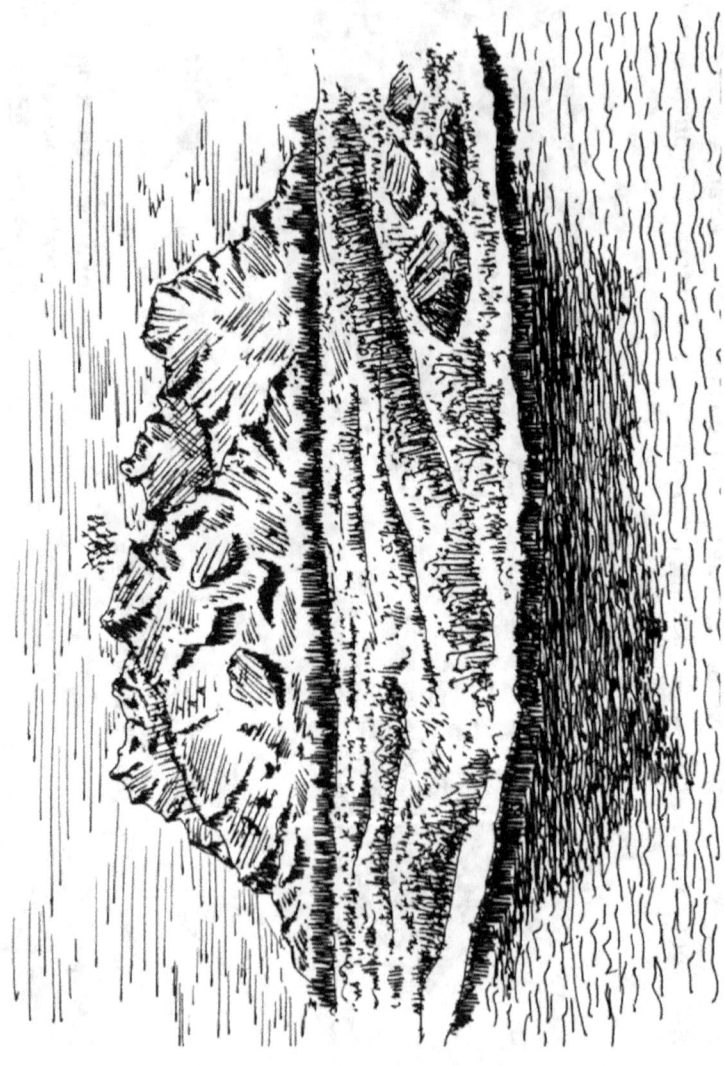

Drawing Water Flowing Towards Viewer:

Instead of water stroke across the page, using following stroke to indicate water flowing outwards towards the viewer.

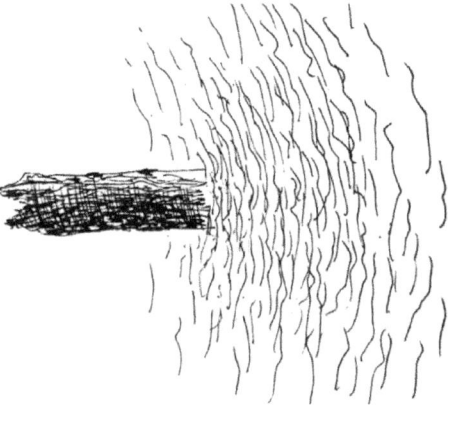

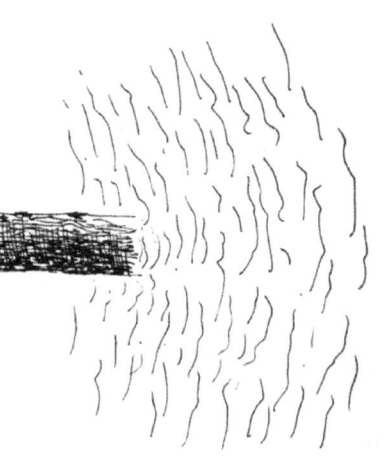

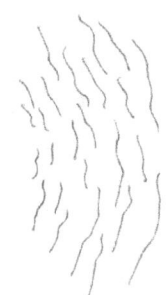

This stroke indicates 'ripples' flowing outwards.

Increase the size as the ripples go away from the object.

Start by drawing the 'ripples' extending out.

Use more ripple stroke for the reflection.

Continued on next page

For more information visit www.pendrawings.me/getstarted

Drawing Water Flowing Towards Viewer:

Direction of lines used for water stroke conveys the sense of direction of flow of water. Same principle is used to draw a river/stream later.

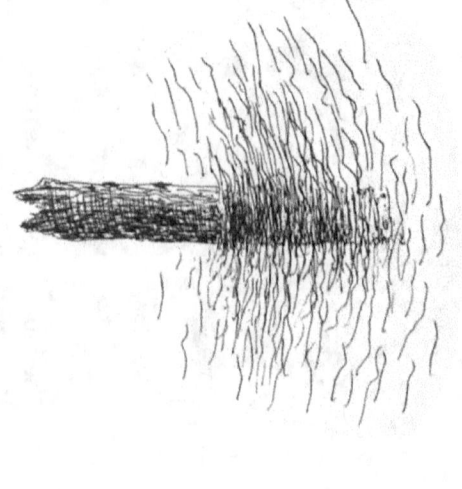

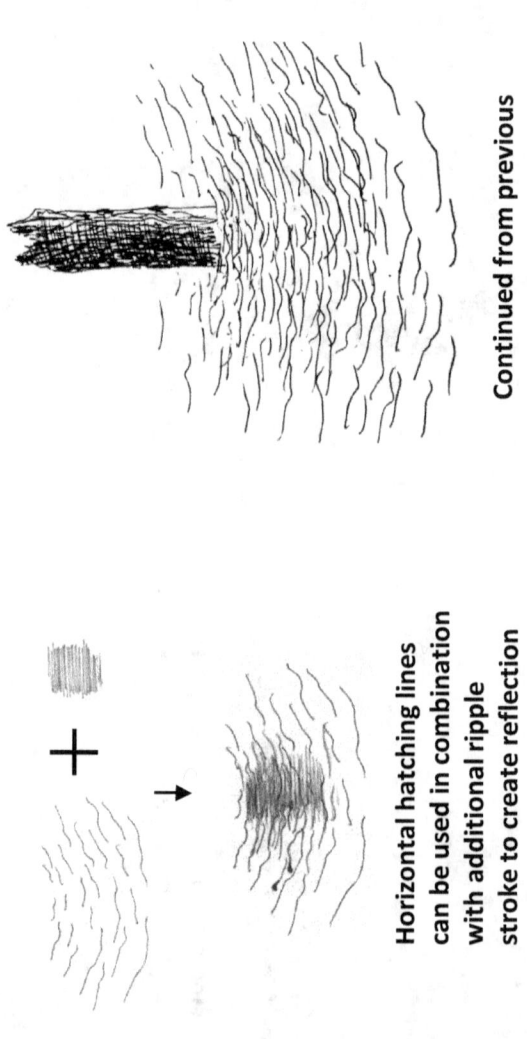

Horizontal hatching lines can be used in combination with additional ripple stroke to create reflection

Continued from previous page.

Add more water stroke and horizontal hatching lines to bring out the reflection.

For more information visit www.pendrawings.me/getstarted

Drawing Water Flowing Towards Viewer:

In an alternate approach, reflection can be drawn initially using horizontal hatching lines and then water stroke added.

Hatching lines like these can be used to indicate a reflection. Ripple stroke can further be added to darken the reflection and indicate water.

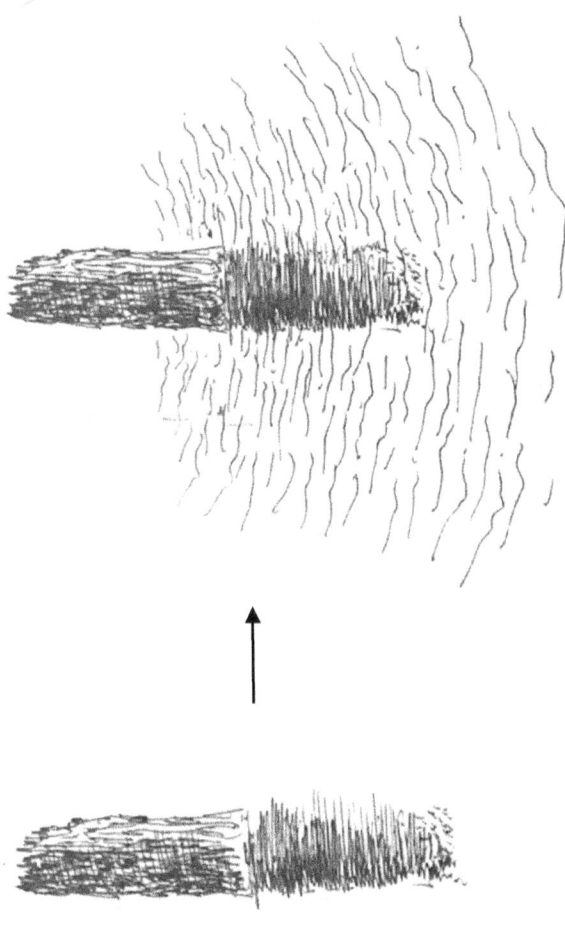

Reflection using hatching lines is drawn first.

Ripple stroke is added next.

For more information visit www.pendrawings.me/getstarted

Activity Drawing Turbulent Water:

Indicate turbulent water flowing across and towards the viewer in the following posts. Draw some of your own.

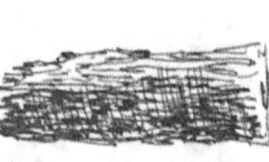

For more information visit www.pendrawings.me/getstarted

Drawing Water Falling Down:

Falling water can be easily indicated by flowing lines as shown below. Add some dots to represent mist.

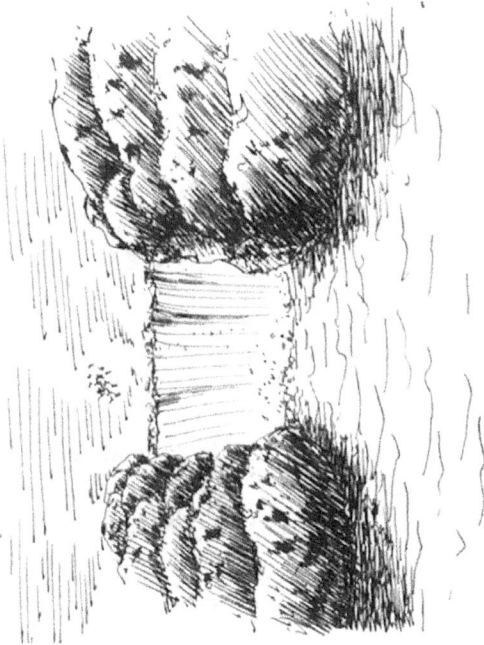

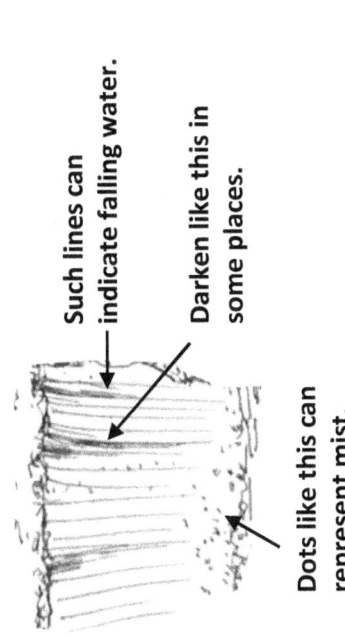

Such lines can indicate falling water.

Darken like this in some places.

Dots like this can represent mist.

Here is a simple drawing. Drawing Stone embankment is covered in another volume.

Drawing Water Falling Down:

Here are some more examples of water falling down. Such drawings can be done quickly and are always fun to do.

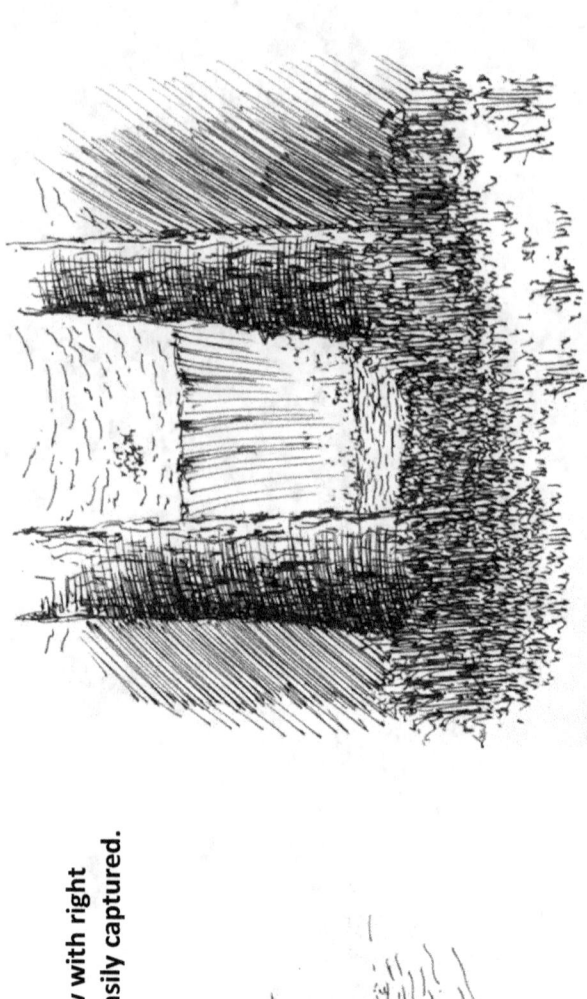

Following drawing shows how with right stroke, falling water can be easily captured.

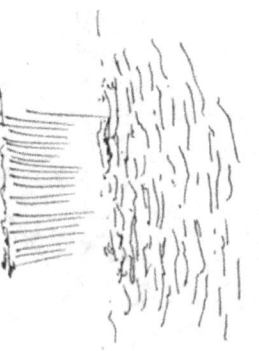

For more information visit www.pendrawings.me/getstarted

Drawing Water Falling Down:

Here is a simple pleasing drawing with water falling down and gently flowing over stones. By using different configuration of stones, different variations on this drawing can be done from imagination any time.

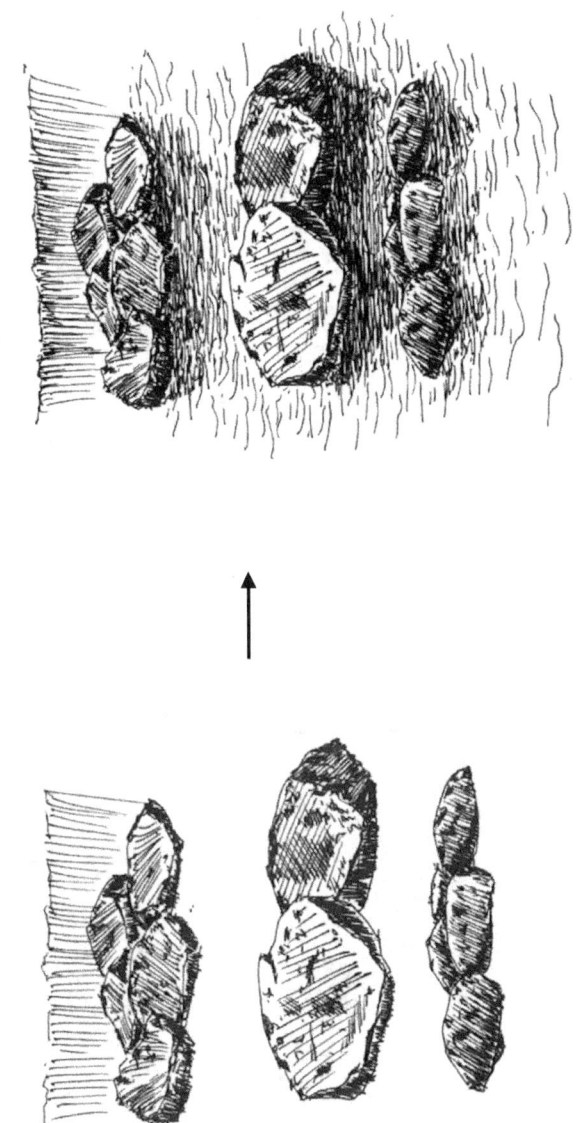

Drawing Cascading Water:

Cascading water, i.e. water falling in multiple levels, can be drawn using the same techniques by creating a pattern of fall, flow, fall, flow etc. as shown below.

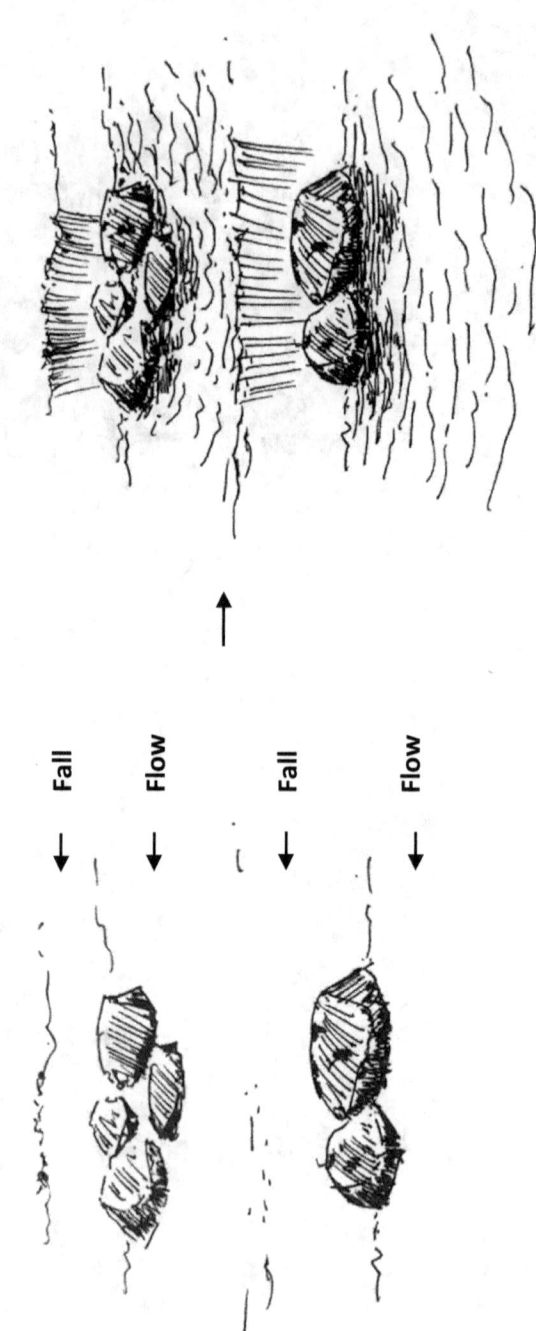

Fall

Flow

Fall

Flow

Drawing a River/Stream:

A river can be indicated by extending the water stroke we learned before to depict the shape of a river. Study the drawing below.

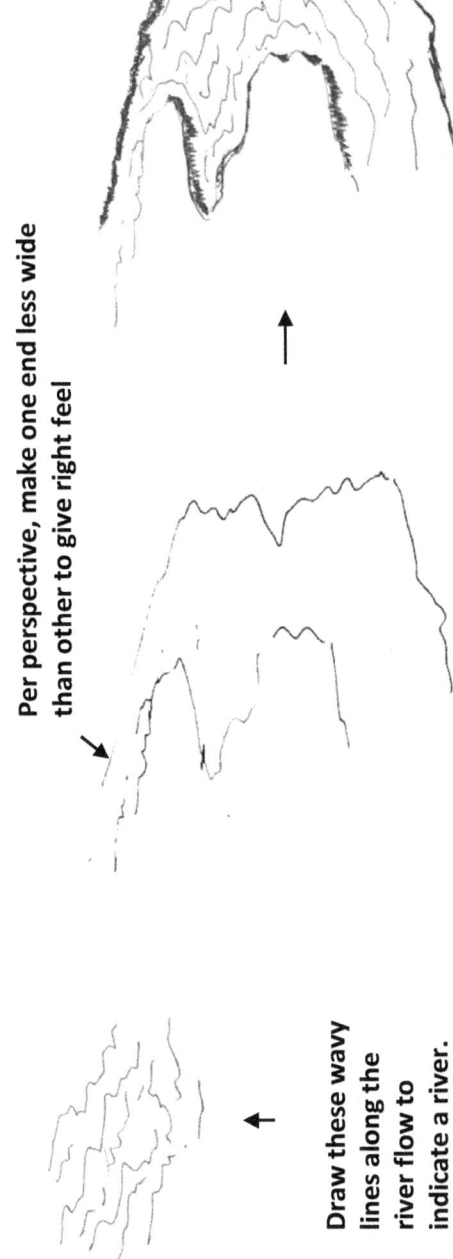

Per perspective, make one end less wide than other to give right feel

Draw these wavy lines along the river flow to indicate a river.

1. Start by drawing a pleasing outline of a river.

2. Add depth to edges and use the stroke indicated to depict a feel of river.

Drawing a River/Stream, Continued:

Draw the lines to convey sense of water movement. Use combination of longer and shorter lines. Keep them wavy to indicate water movement.

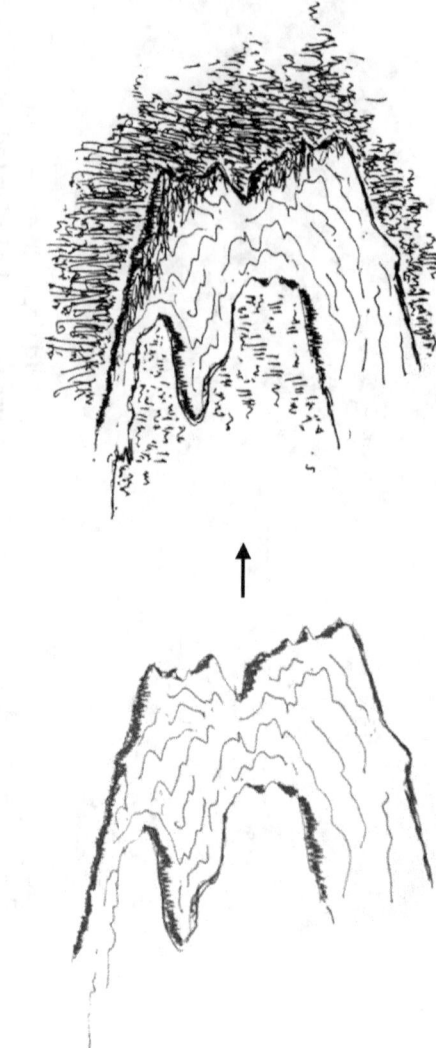

In the absence of color, a reflection is very helpful in reinforcing feel of water. Add a foliage or other elements with appropriate reflections to bring out the desired feel of water.

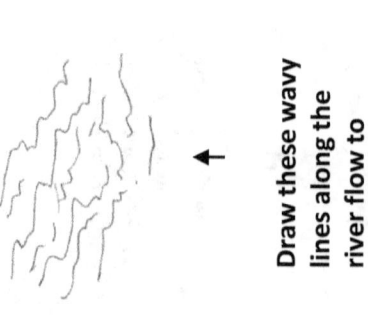

Draw these wavy lines along the river flow to indicate a river

Drawing a River, Another Example:

Following is another example of drawing a river. Notice the tapered shape and use of flowing lines to give feel of water.

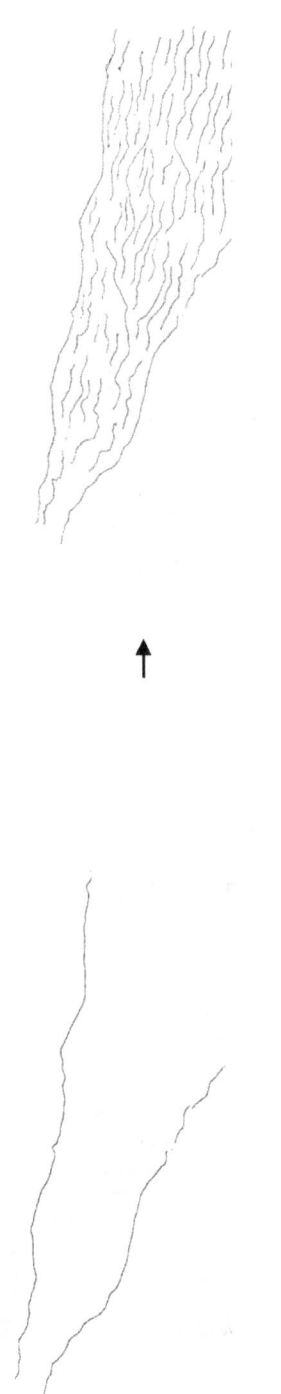

Use such flowing lines to give indication of water.

Use of such tapered shape gives more perception of depth.

Drawing a River, Another Example, Continued:

Reflection is indicated by use of more water stroke to increase tone. Notice irregular darkening of reflection to indicate water flow. With river in foreground, pine trees provide a nice contrast in middle ground. Though I haven't done it here, a backdrop of mountain can be used as well.

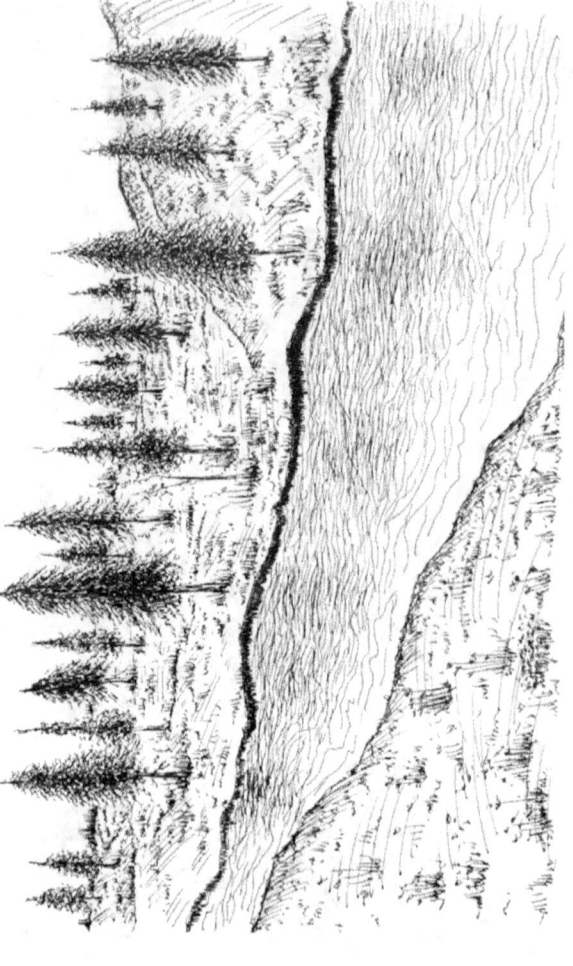

Drawing a River/Stream, Continued:

Here are some more examples. Such simple pleasing drawings can be easily drawn in between your short breaks and helps to quickly build your confidence with pen and ink drawing.

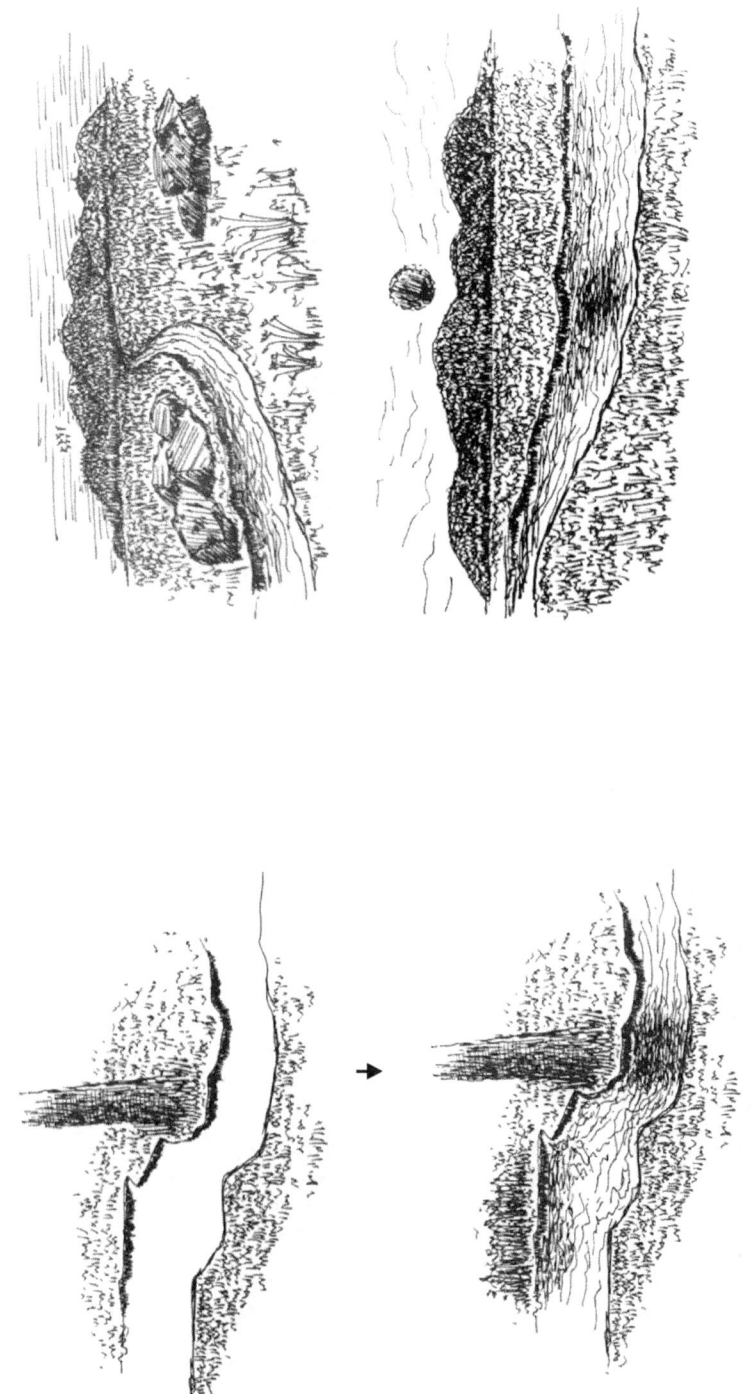

Drawing Water Flowing between Stones:

Water flowing between stone embankment is a very pleasing composition that can be used in many setting like in a stream flowing through woods as in the following example. Always start by drawing stones first. Drawing them is covered in detail in vol. 3 of my pen and ink drawing workbooks.

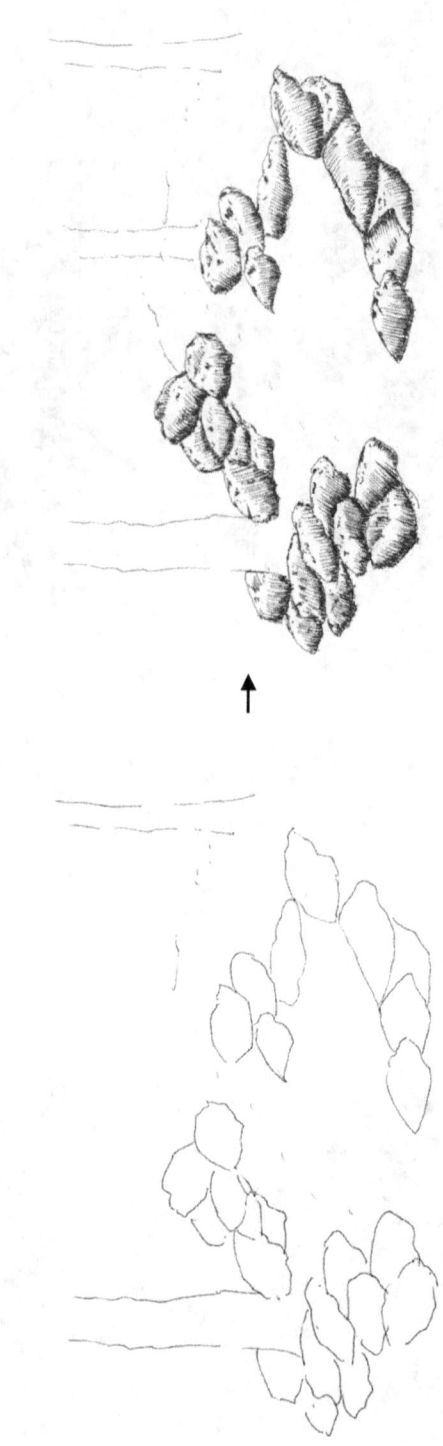

Start by laying out stones and texturing them. This sets up the space to fill with water.

Drawing Water Flowing between Stones, Continued:

It is very important to make edges of reflection irregular in moving water. Use tonal variation with darker tone near stones to indicate reflection.

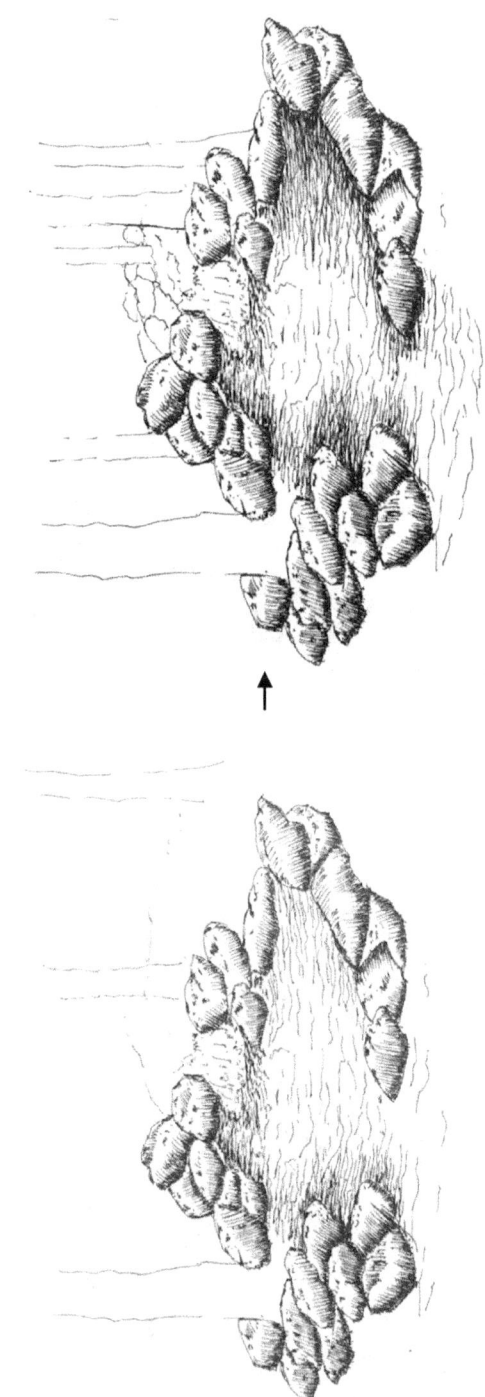

Add water stroke as discussed earlier. Use more tone near stones with irregular outline to indicate reflection.

For more information visit www.pendrawings.me/getstarted

Drawing Water Flowing between Stones, Finished:

Tonal variation in reflection can be added with very dark tone next to stones and slightly lighter tone bit away from them. This adds to bit of realism. Other elements are textured to finish this quick drawing.

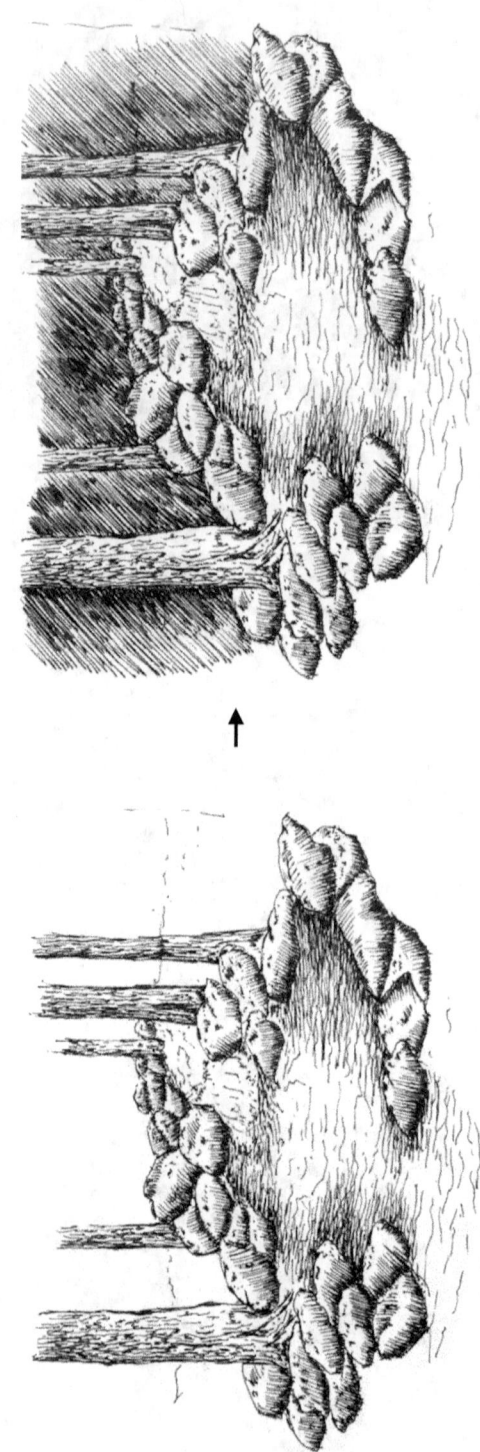

Always maintain contrast in your drawing. Above, the darker surroundings are contrasted against the lighter tone of stones. The reflection contrasts well with the lighter tone in the center of water.

Activity: Finish the Following Outline per earlier instructions

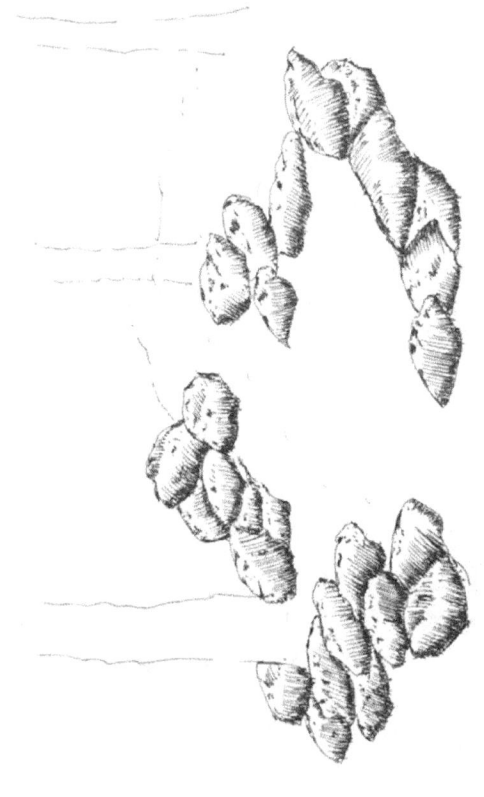

Combining a Stream & Waterfall:

A stream and waterfall can be combined to create very pleasing compositions. A waterfall can be source of a stream as shown below, or a stream can lead to a waterfall.

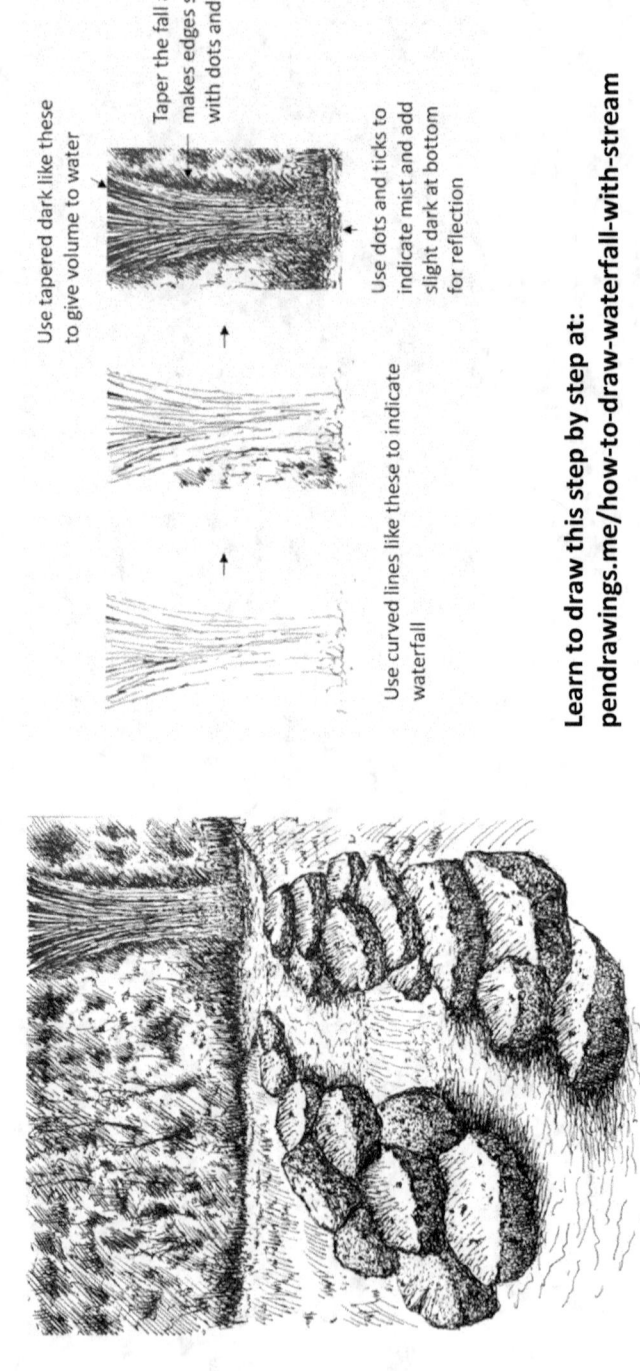

Use tapered dark like these to give volume to water

Taper the fall and makes edges softer with dots and ticks

Use dots and ticks to indicate mist and add slight dark at bottom for reflection

Use curved lines like these to indicate waterfall

**Learn to draw this step by step at:
pendrawings.me/how-to-draw-waterfall-with-stream**

Drawing a Wave:

A wave is characterized by water movement in successive layers. To indicate more water, darken a layer as shown below

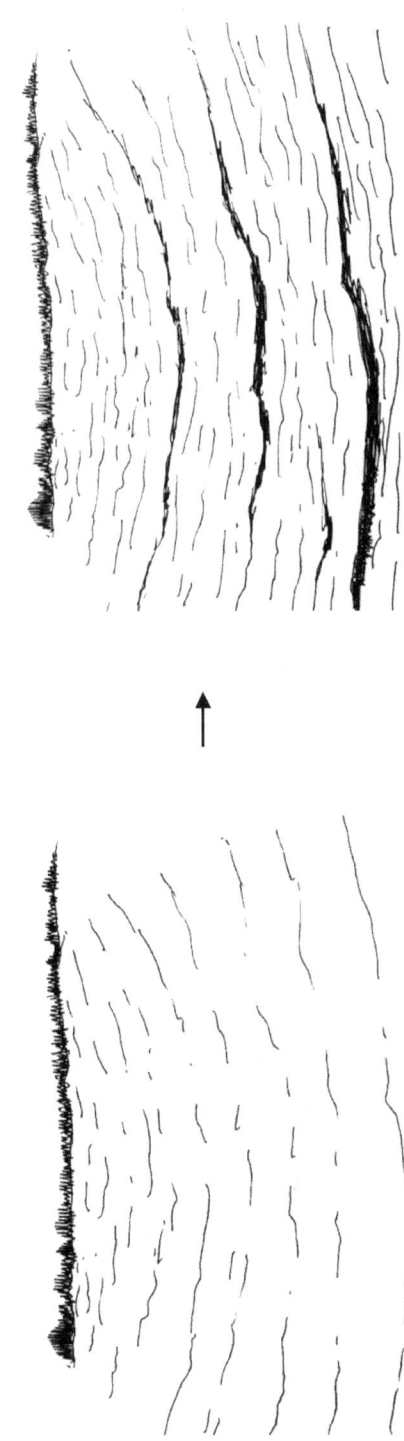

Wave gains in size closer to viewer and hence make the darker area bigger closer to viewer. They also open, or flatten, as they go out closer to viewer. Also avoid a regular line. Instead use slightly irregular lines for waves as shown above.

Other Examples of Drawing Water:

There are limitless ways in which water can be incorporated in a drawing. Following are some more examples. By using techniques you have learned so far, these can be attempted.

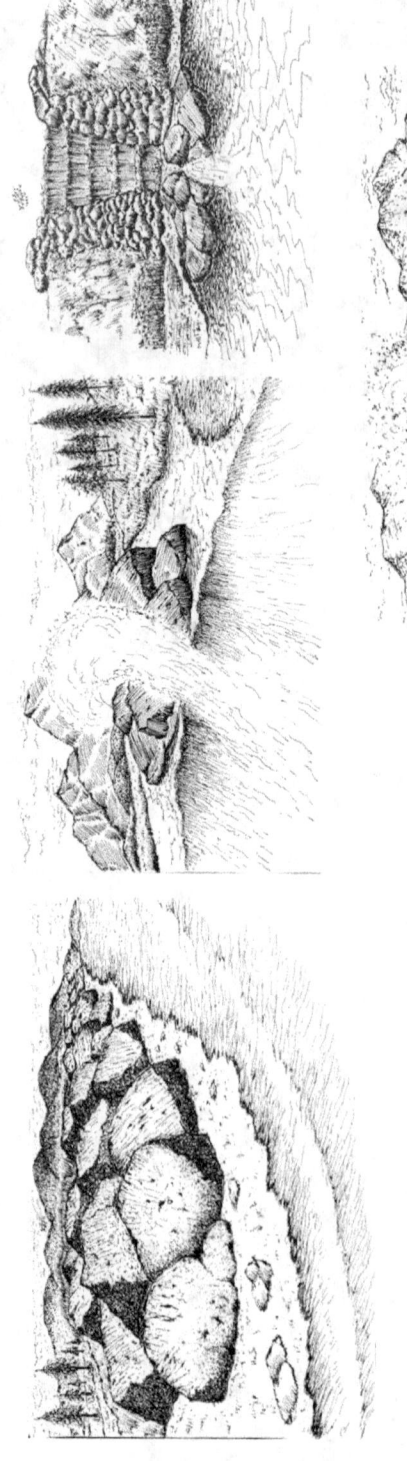

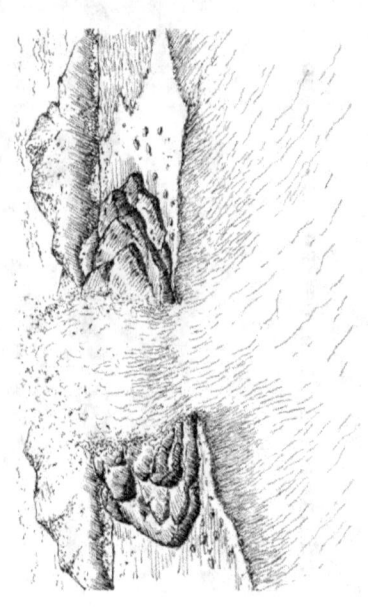

To learn to draw them step by step, pl. visit:
pendrawings.me/step-by-step-easy-pen-and-ink-drawings

For more information visit www.pendrawings.me/getstarted

Drawing Wooden Structure:

A wooden structure like a wooden house, barn, log cabin etc. can add charm to any drawing. Once the technique to draw wooden slats is understood, any kind of wooden structure comprised of wooden slats can be drawn.

It is very important to keep perspective in mind when drawing outline of a wooden structure as only a wooden structure drawn in perspective looks plausible. It takes practice in the beginning, but once understood, is becomes very easy to draw a wooden structure in perspective.

A wooden structure is usually in the foreground in a drawing. Simple compositions with wooden structure consists of a wooden structure in foreground with other foreground element like trees, stones etc. with a backdrop of a mountain or hill. A wooden structure with river flowing across with its reflection in water is also a pleasing composition that can be attempted.

Drawing a Wooden Structure:

A wooden structure is comprised of wooden slats. Following is the technique to draw a wooden slat. Use short overlapping hatching lines to give it a base tone and finish with tapered crevices to give it a wooden feel.

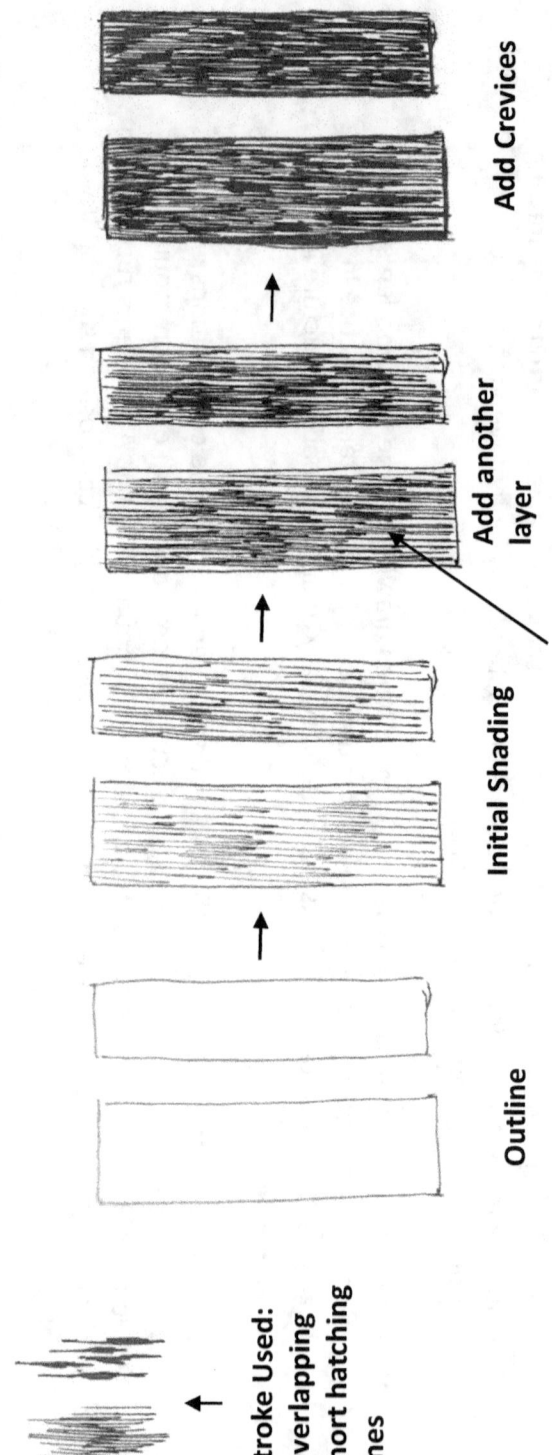

Stroke Used:
Overlapping
short hatching
lines

Outline

Initial Shading

Add another layer

Add Crevices

Overlapping lines create darker areas which creates feel of wooden texture

For more information visit www.pendrawings.me/getstarted

Drawing a Wooden Structure, continued:

Following are simple steps to draw a wooden structure. In the outline, indicate the slats and texture them per earlier instructions to give it a wooden feel.

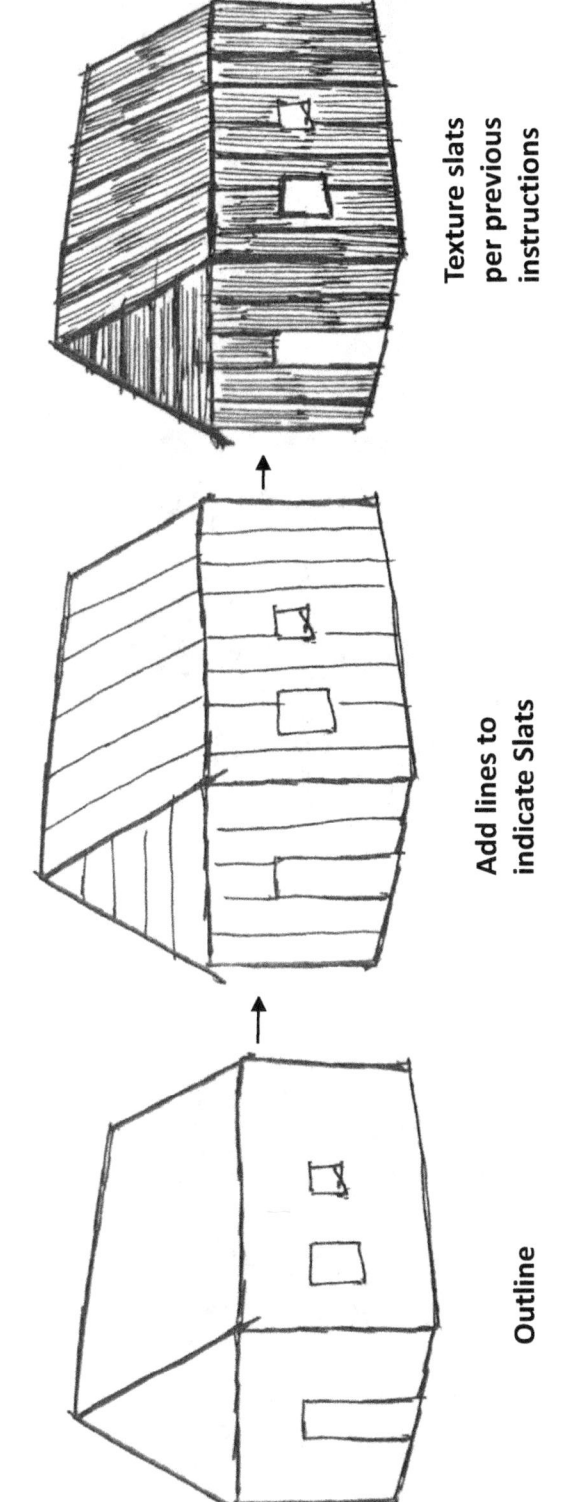

Outline

Add lines to indicate Slats

Texture slats per previous instructions

For more information visit www.pendrawings.me/getstarted

Drawing a Wooden Structure, continued:

Just like with mountains, one side should be made darker than the other per concept of tonal variation. Add ground cover and a background element to create a pleasing drawing.

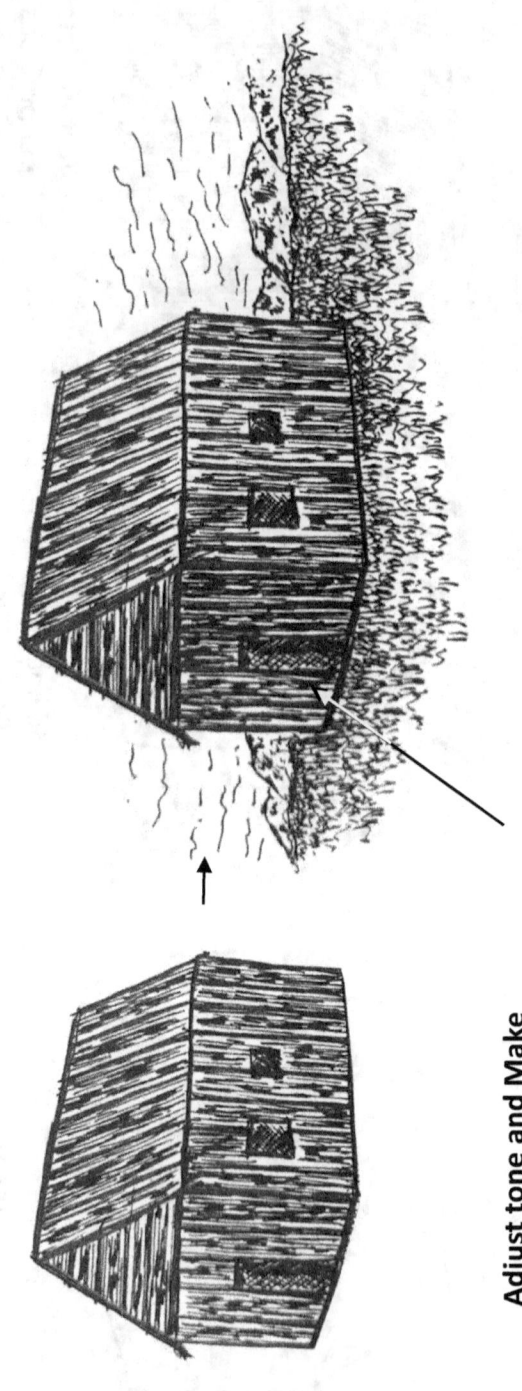

Adjust tone and Make doors and windows darker

Make this side bit darker assuming Sun is behind the house

Finish with other elements

Drawing Outline of Structure in Perspective:

Drawing the structure in perspective is very important otherwise it appears wrong. In perspective, the edge closer to viewer is bigger than the edge away from the viewer.

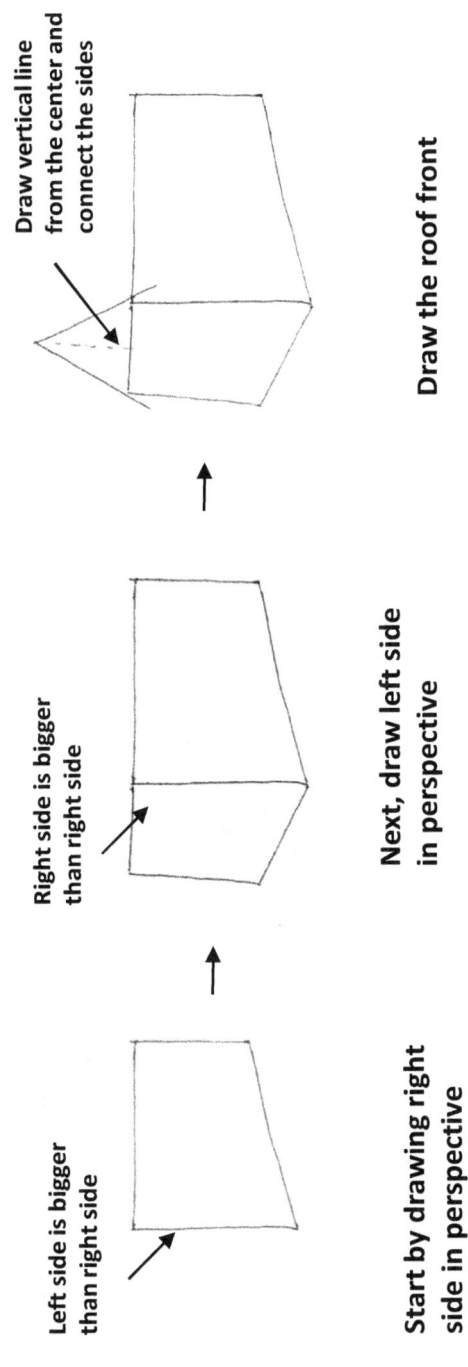

Left side is bigger than right side

Right side is bigger than right side

Draw vertical line from the center and connect the sides

Start by drawing right side in perspective

Next, draw left side in perspective

Draw the roof front

For more information visit www.pendrawings.me/getstarted

Drawing Outline of Structure in Perspective, continued:

As a general perspective rule, for any side, the vertical edge closer to viewer is bigger than the edge away from the viewer.

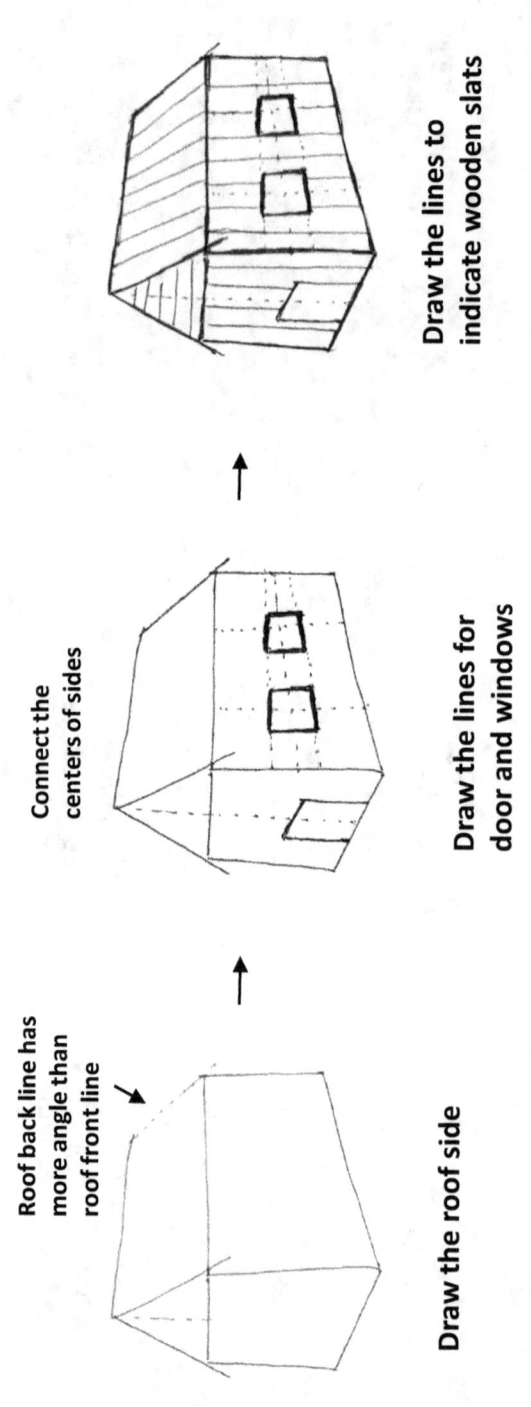

Roof back line has
more angle than
roof front line

Draw the roof side

Connect the
centers of sides

Draw the lines for
door and windows

Draw the lines to
indicate wooden slats

Pl. visit www.pendrawings.me/perspective for more detailed explanation on perspective as it applies to drawing.

Landscapes with Wooden Structure:

A wooden structure in the foreground with a nice background element is a simple pleasing composition that can be attempted anytime.

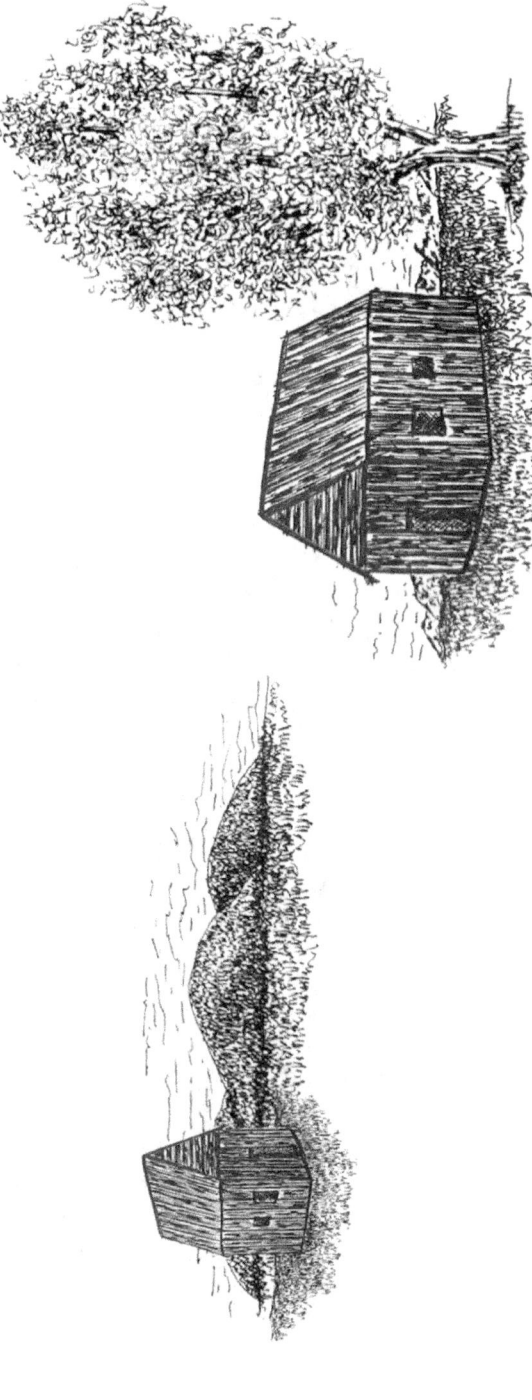

You can look for images of barns and other wooden structures in Google or other search engines and use them in your drawings as well. Old Barns have a very special appeal that you can make part of your drawing.

Here is an example of a drawing with a Barn:

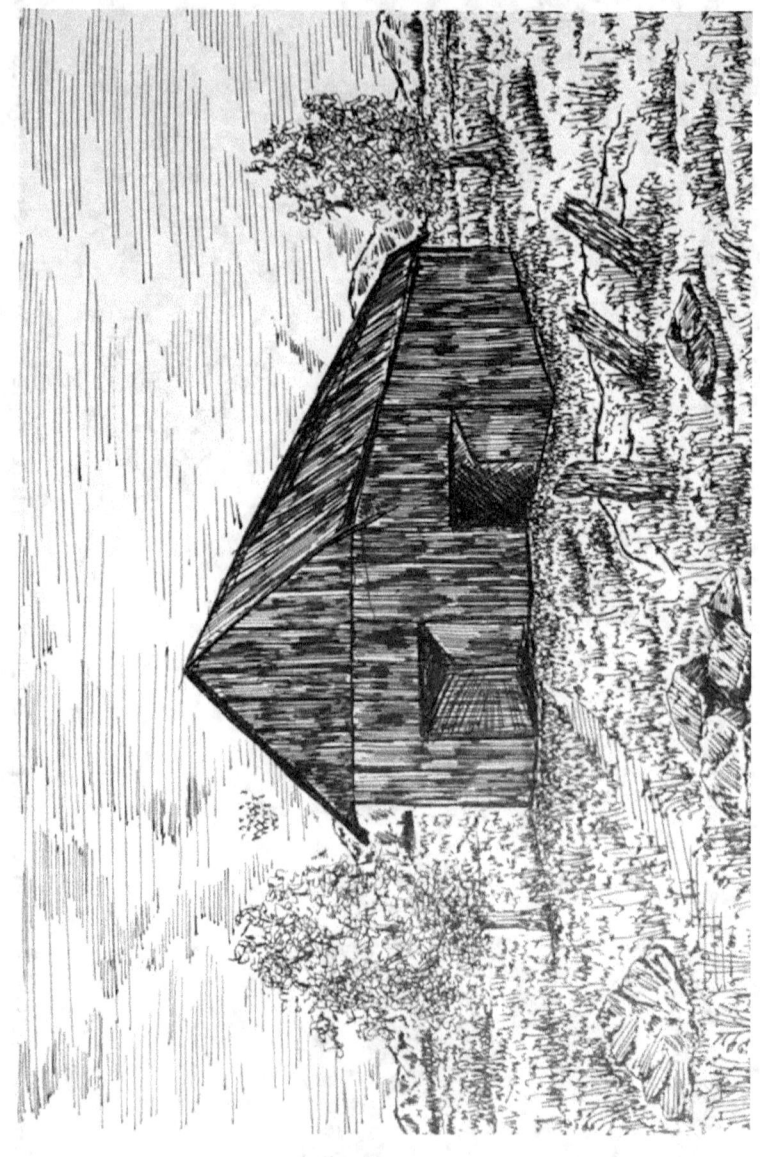

This completes this workbook but hopefully this is just the beginning of your pen and ink drawing adventure. You can visit my website for completely free tutorials and use other workbooks I have created to learn how to draw other elements of nature, like trunks, stones etc. with pen and ink and create more interesting landscapes.

www.pendrawings.me/workbooks

Practice is key to improving. Carry a small pocket sketch book with you and a pen and try to draw something when ever you get some time. If you don't like your initial attempt, try again. Don't get discouraged.

Any comments, suggestions and feedback on improving contents of this workbook are most welcome. For more information on drawing landscapes with pen and ink, to learn more about my works and to reach me, please visit my website.

www.pendrawings.me/getstarted

Happy drawing,

Rahul Jain

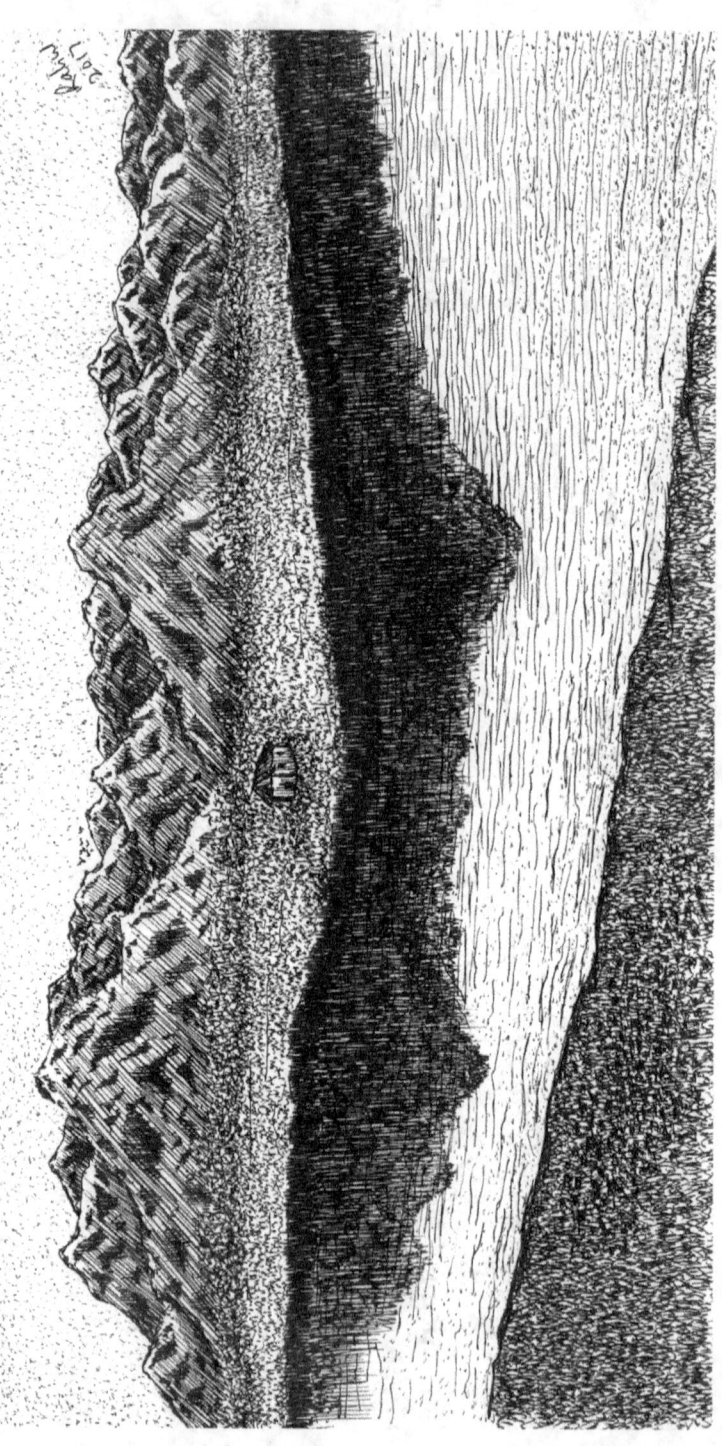

Away form it all : Copyright: Rahul Jain

God's Own Land: Copyright: Rahul Jain

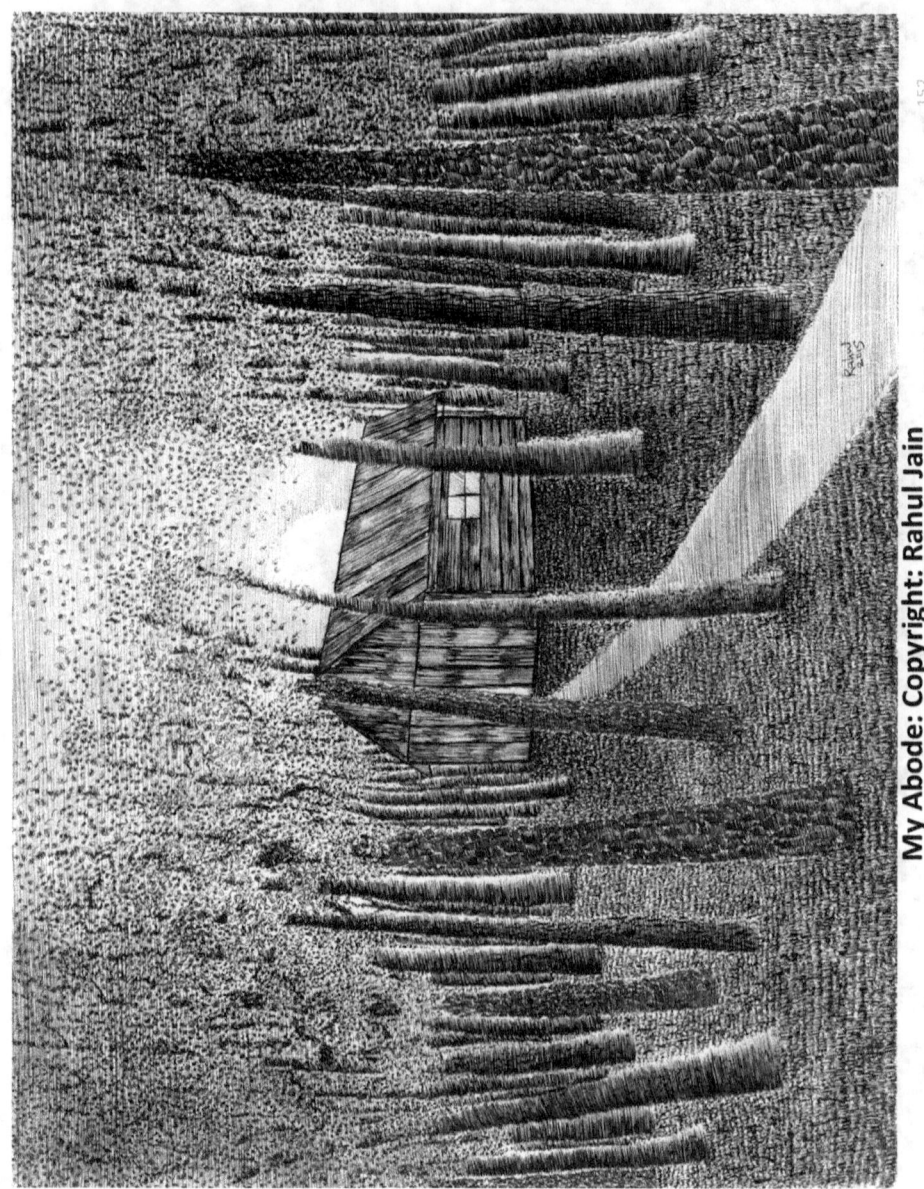

My Abode: Copyright: Rahul Jain

My Refuge: Copyright: Rahul Jain

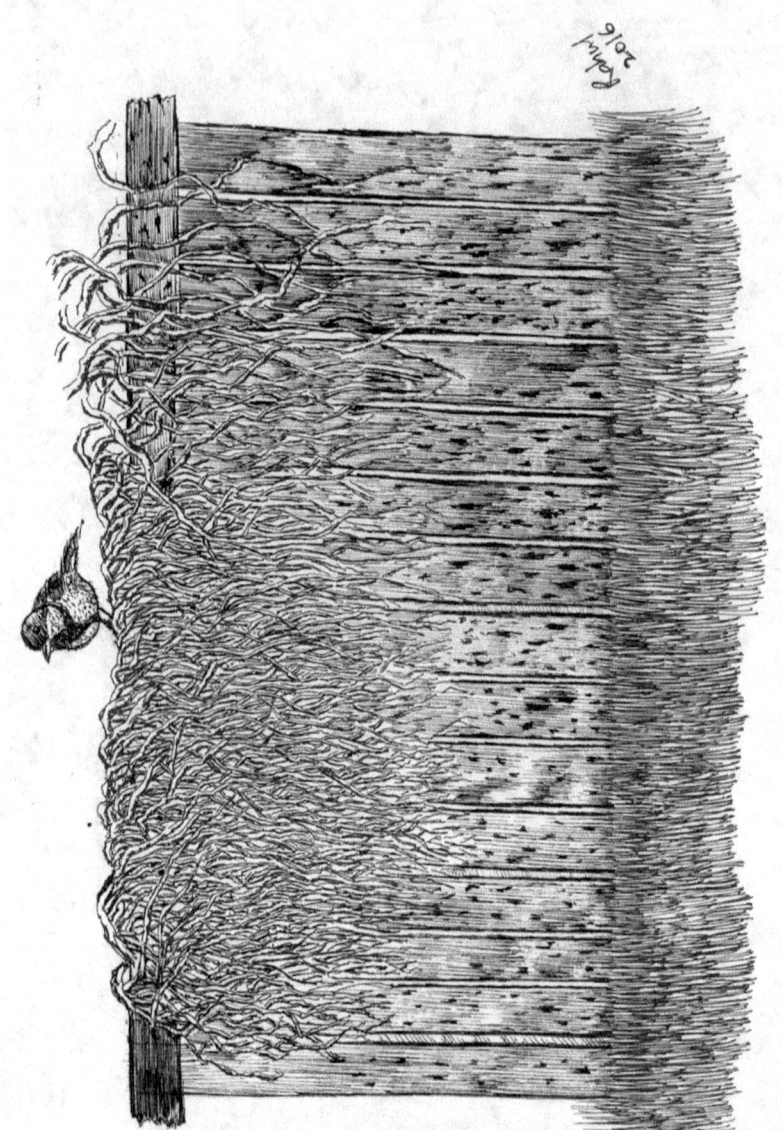

Fence: Copyright: Rahul Jain